TANNY McGREGOR

Genre Connections

Lessons to Launch Literary and Nonfiction Texts

HEINEMANN
Portsmouth, NH

Heinemann
361 Hanover Street
Portsmouth, NH 03801–3912
www.heinemann.com

Offices and agents throughout the world

The author and publisher wish to thank those who have generously given permission to reprint borrowed material in this book:

Excerpt from *I Had Trouble in Getting to Solla Sollew* by Dr. Seuss, Trademark™ and Copyright © by Dr. Seuss Enterprises, L. P. 1965, renewed 1993. Used by permission of Random House Children's Books, a division of Random House, Inc. Any third-party use of this material, outside of this publication, is prohibited. Interested parties must apply directly to Random House, Inc., for permission.

Library of Congress Cataloging-in-Publication Data
McGregor, Tanny.
   Genre connections : lessons to launch literary and nonfiction texts /
Tanny McGregor.
      pages cm
   Includes bibliographical references and index.
   ISBN-13: 978-0-325-03396-9
   1. Literary form—Study and teaching. 2. Youth—Books and reading. 3. Reading comprehension. I. Title.
   LB1575.M34 2013
   372.64'044—dc23
                          2012045494

Editors: Harvey "Smokey" Daniels *and* Tobey Antao
Production: Patty Adams
Cover and Interior Photographs: Brynne McGregor, Miles McGregor, Tanny McGregor, and Rachel Ryba
Cover and Interior Designs: Monica Ann Crigler
Typesetter: Gina Poirier Design
Manufacturing: Steve Bernier

Printed in the United States of America on acid-free paper
17 16 15 14 13 VP 2 3 4 5

To Graycie, my feline companion of eighteen years.

Her dreams of becoming a published author are realized here,
even if posthumously.

"/"""""""""";;u=[]* ?hyt5-t"

Contents

Acknowledgments

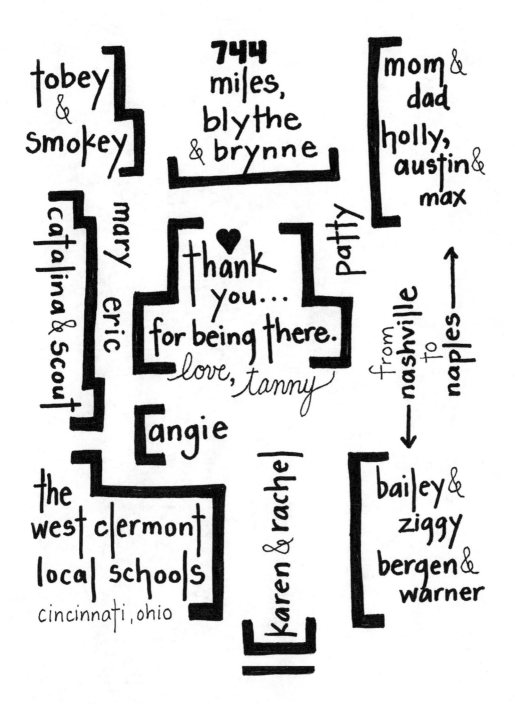

tobey & smokey

744 miles, blythe & brynne

mom & dad holly, austin & max

catalina & scout

mary

eric

❤ thank you... for being there.

love, tanny

patty

from nashville to naples →

angie

the west clermont local schools
cincinnati, ohio

karen & rachel

bailey & ziggy bergen & warner

Prologue
My First Book

I'm glad you're considering reading this book. Honored, really. I mean, you are a busy person and there are a million other books you could choose to read. But as much as I hope you enjoy what you find here and put it to good use with your students, I can't help but wish you'd read my first book, first. I know it sounds ungrateful to say that. Like a sales ploy, even. To know why I think an understanding of genre is important, though, you've got to see where my thinking began.

Thankfully, Tobey and Smokey, my gracious editors, are allowing me to share my first book with you, right here, right now. And no, I'm not talking about *Comprehension Connections* (2007) or *Comprehension Going Forward* (2011). The book I'm talking about was written long before either of those. My first book is, by far, the most important book I've ever written. It is the book that made me an author.

Writing my first book taught me more than all of the other pieces I've written since. I learned that words have power. I learned that people who might not listen to you when you talk *will* listen to you when you write. I learned that I could write about elephants or Easter eggs or anything I wanted. I didn't know it then, but I was learning about genre.

```
                THE LITTLEST ELEPHANT




         WRITTEN AND ILLUSTRATED BY




             TANYA WILLIAMSON
```

The Littlest Elephant, Written and Illustrated by Tanya (Tanny) Williamson (McGregor) Miss Hendel's Kindergarten Class, 1971

One day a very little elephant was born.

His father didn't act like he cared very much about him.

One day all of the elephants held on to each others tails and walked in a line.

     The Littlest Elephant wasn't the only book I wrote in 1971. And fiction wasn't the only genre. I also wrote *The Easter Egg Hunt* (a memoir) and *James' Birthday Party* (nonfiction). I tried out genres the way a chemist experiments with substances or a composer plays around with melodies. I remember feeling like a different person with each new genre I tried. When I wrote fiction, I felt free and creative, like no rules applied to me. When I wrote nonfiction, I felt like a reporter who had to get the facts right so others could learn from me. And around this same time, in 1970 and 1971, I was listening to and learning to read different genres and noticing how they made me feel . . . so lucky was I to have a mother and a kindergarten teacher who immersed me in all sorts of text.

But the little elephant couldn't hold on.

Then one day he got stung by a bee. He didn't cry. He just said to the bee, "Get off."

Since he was so brave they made him king of the elephants.
THE END

Like author Randy Bomer says, "Genre seems to be a psychological necessity for starting to write or read" (2003). I know it was for me. The better I understood the personality of the type of text I was writing or reading, the more meaningful the experience. And I'm still learning about those text personalities, even in the writing of this book.

It has been more than four decades since I wrote my first book. I've learned a lot about genre since then, and much of that learning is contained in this volume. For me, no book could ever top *The Littlest Elephant*, but I promise I gave it a royal try.

Tanny McGregor
Cincinnati, Ohio
2013

A Very Good Place to Start

Good instruction is a mingling of *why* and *how*. The *why* mixes rationale and research. The *how* combines engagement and creativity with everyday classroom instruction. I'll be honest: I sometimes rush through the why to get to the how. I just can't wait for the thrill of trying something new with my students, to give them, as Leonardo da Vinci calls it, "the noblest pleasure . . . the joy of understanding." But I know that I'll teach each lesson with stronger conviction and hold higher expectations for my students if I am confident in the why. Insight about the why leads me away from the flavor-of-the-day kind of instruction, and stops me from considering lessons that lack substance.

The Why

*"In order to become competent, literate members of society,
students must be able to navigate multiple genres.
They need to know how to confidently read, write, and discuss
narrative, informational, persuasive, and analytical texts.
Because these forms of texts are unique and require unique
strategies for reading and writing, it is not safe to assume that
students who are competent with one genre will automatically
master another. Students need to learn about particular genres
through implicit experience and explicit instruction."*

—from *Thinking Through Genre* by Heather Lattimer (2003)

My daughter Brynne puts a face on this quotation. One lazy winter afternoon at our house, during a span of about three hours, I watched Brynne navigate multiple genres, either for entertainment, necessity, or both. She read an iPhone manual, a novel titled *Miss Peregrine's Home for Peculiar Children*, an Internet article about feline health, a few movie reviews, the menu on the Chipotle app, and a brochure containing safety guidelines for a space heater. Some of these she comprehended with ease, while others required slower, more deliberate reading, prompting her to ask questions along the way. Just like me, Brynne is more competent with some types of text than with others. Right before my eyes, however, she is becoming more and more prepared for the diverse and complex reading that lies ahead.

The Common Core State Standards (CCSS) echo this emphasis. In the College and Career Readiness Anchor Standards for Reading, a note on the range and content of student reading speaks out loud and clear:

> To build a foundation for college and career readiness, students must read widely and deeply from among a broad range of high-quality, increasingly challenging literary and informational texts. Through extensive reading of stories, dramas, poems, and myths from diverse cultures and different time periods, students gain literary and cultural knowledge as well as familiarity with various text structures and elements. By reading texts in history/social studies, science, and other disciplines, students build a foundation of knowledge in these fields that will also give them the background to be better readers in all content areas. Students can only gain this foundation when the curriculum is intentionally and coherently structured to develop rich content knowledge within and across grades. Students also acquire the habits of reading independently and closely, which are essential to their future success.

Our students will get implicit experience with various genres as they go about living their twenty-first-century lives. The explicit instruction, however, must come from you and me. The remaining chapters in this book are a collection of ideas about how to launch genres, how to introduce your students to the unique personalities of each, and how to build a curiosity and appreciation for what each genre has to offer. There are dozens of genres on the continuum between narrative (story) and expository (informational); this book will explore but a few. Any genre could be launched using the model in this book, however, like realistic fiction, mystery, or technical writing, for example. Use the seed ideas suggested in this volume with a genre of your choice and see how it grows!

The How

How do we take an abstract concept like genre and make it accessible and interesting to our students? How can we pique their interest in types of text and move them into being readers and writers of multiple genres? The launching sequence from *Comprehension Connections*, which ushers our students into an understanding of the thinking strategies, can help us here. As I state on pages four and five: "I didn't set out to create a formulaic path to follow for the launching of a strategy, but upon reflection, I discovered some instructional patterns had emerged. This launching sequence was born from trial and error and a lot of talk with teachers."

With the use of concrete objects, art, music, and short samples of text, we can launch a genre study or simply acquaint students with a genre's personality. And along the way, we'll allow for plenty of time for talk. It's fair to say that these ideas shape my thinking when planning to teach any abstract topic or concept, whether it be genres, thinking strategies, social studies, or science concepts . . . you name it. Let's define terms.

- **Launching sequence:** A progression for planning lessons that honors the gradual release of responsibility. This sequence allows time for teacher modeling, thinking aloud, and lots of talk. Kids acquire and practice the language of the genre, having fun along the way!

- **Concrete experience:** An initial exposure to a genre, a lesson with a concrete focus. Connections are easily made, creating bridges of thinking from the known to the new. Concrete lessons anchor future thinking.

- **Notice and name the genre:** A time for students to inquire and explore with the genre.

LAUNCHING SEQUENCE

concrete experience

notice and name the genre

sensory exercise

read to learn about the genre

time for text

- **Sensory exercise:** A lesson that links the concrete experience to new thinking, providing opportunities to learn through music and art.

- **Read to learn about the genre:** An experience where students learn about the genre from the genre.

- **Quotations to get kids talking:** A thought-provoking collection of quotations from authors, artists, musicians, and other great thinkers that spurs our students to consider the power of genres beyond the walls of the classroom.

- **Time for text:** A bibliography of resources for teachers who have enjoyed the launching sequence and are ready to guide their students into exploration of a genre.

The launching sequence has breathed new life into my teaching and has made learning more incremental and accessible for my students. When I step back and take a broader look, I realize it is powered by the use of metaphor. I wholeheartedly agree with Rick Wormelli, author of *Metaphors and Analogies: Power Tools for Teaching Any Subject* (Stenhouse, 2009): "There is nothing in the K–12 curriculum that is so symbolic or abstract that we could not create a physical comparison that would sharpen students' understanding." As you'll see, I compare poetry to a jar, historical fiction to a clothespin, and autobiography to a mirror, just to name a few. I've seen the abstract concepts of genre come alive for students when I tap into the limitless influence of metaphor.

Each part of the launching sequence is important, but let's zoom in on the two steps where metaphor fuels the capacity for deeper understanding: the concrete experience and the sensory exercise.

The Concrete Experience:
Make It Real

"The more interesting, intense, and concrete the experiences
accessed or built through frontloading, the better for the reader."
—Jeffrey Wilhelm

If my pastor introduces a sermon with a concrete object, I am more likely to listen intently and then, later in the week, think about the sermon and it's application to my life. Recently when I entered the sanctuary to my church, I noticed a weightlifting bench and some free weights sitting on the stage. I was instantly curious about how these objects would connect with the theme of the church service and I began making inferences. Thanks to a few concrete objects, I was thinking about the sermon before it even started. Days later, I found myself thinking about how resistance can make us stronger. My pastor would be proud. His instructional design worked.

I'm not the only one who responds openly and instantly to concrete lessons. Time and time again I've seen it happen with my students, from preschool to high school, and in professional development sessions with teachers, too. In *Made to Stick* (Random House, 2007), authors Chip and Dan Heath say that of all the ways we can try to make learning long-lasting, "concreteness is perhaps the easiest to embrace." It works. And not just for the kids who are reading well and seem to learn everything with ease. It also works for kids who are struggling in reading, who do not usually respond to abstract concepts, texts, and mundane paper/pencil tasks. Our students who are learning English can easily latch on to these concrete launching lessons, as well. Objects from everyday life, with no text attached, level the playing field and allow for valuable thinking time for everyone in the room. The Heath brothers go on to say, "Language is often abstract, but *life* is not abstract." And later, in their chapter titled "Concreteness": "Abstraction makes it harder to understand an idea and to remember it. It also makes it harder to coordinate our activities with others, who may interpret the abstraction in very different ways. Concreteness helps us avoid these problems."

In her 2008 *Educational Leadership* article, "The Object of Their Attention," Dr. Shari Tishman from Harvard's Project Zero builds a case for concrete objects. Tishman states:

> Concrete objects are also engaging and accessible, especially in a group setting. You'll find that once students start generating observations and ideas about an object, it's hard to get them to stop. This is because looking carefully at something and trying to discern its features is a form of cognition with an intrinsically re-warding feedback loop. The more you look, the more you see; the more you see, the more interesting the object becomes. Moreover, examining objects directly—either visually, tactually, or aurally— is something most students can do. Regardless of background knowledge, learning style, or skill, almost all students can notice features of an object, ask questions about it, and generate ideas and connections. Students' responses may differ, but these differ-ences contribute to the conversation rather than detract from it.

One of the most powerful parts of the launching sequence is the concrete experience. When I plan for instruction (and I'm not necessarily talking about sitting at a desk when I'm planning . . . it's more often when I'm driving or walking or putting away laundry), I look for creative ways to use objects to maximize engagement and understanding.

The Sensory Exercise: Come to Understand Through Art and Music

Art and music. Sometimes nothing else will do.

It's like when the doors to your house are locked and you can't find your keys. You have to search for other ways to get inside, ways that you might not have considered before, ways that might not be as easy or as comfortable. That's what art and music can do. They provide another way to understand the abstract, a pathway that is pleasurable and metacognitive all at once. Now after more than two decades of building my instructional repertoire, I turn to art and music without delay instead of saving them for my last resort. With some students, I can teach and reteach all day long, but unless I provide a sensory exercise, comprehension is elusive. My students need the images and melodies to intercede, speaking a language that everyone understands. Consider these words from Elliot Eisner and Arthur Costa.

> *"The arts also teach that neither words nor numbers define*
> *the limits of our cognition; we know more than we can tell.*
> *There are many experiences and a multitude of occasions in which*
> *we need art forms to say what literal language cannot say."*
> **—Elliot W. Eisner, emeritus professor of art and education**
> **at Stanford University School of Education**

> *"All information gets to the brain through our sensory channels—*
> *our tactile, gustatory, olfactory, visual, kinesthetic, and auditory*
> *senses. Those whose sensory pathways are open, alert, and acute*
> *absorb more information from the environment than those whose*
> *pathways are withered, immune, and oblivious to sensory stimuli.*
> *It is proposed, therefore, that aesthetics is an essential element of*

*thinking skills programs. Cognitive education should include the
development of sensory acumen."*
**—Arthur L. Costa, emeritus professor of education
at California State University Sacramento**

Using art and music is not an option; it's a necessity. If I tackle an abstract
concept, unit, or chapter and neglect to look through the lens of art and music, I
am sure to leave some students behind.

In the chapters to follow you'll meet (or become reacquainted with) artists like
Joseph Cornell and his Cornell Box. You'll listen to singer/songwriter Mary Chapin
Carpenter and discover the historical content of her lyrics. Along with each new
genre of writing, new genres of art and music are introduced, just waiting to be
enjoyed. And that's an added benefit of sprinkling in art and music as you introduce students to genre: enjoyment. The arts inspire new thinking while providing
simple, essential enjoyment.

*"And while a hundred civilizations have prospered
(sometimes for centuries) without computers or windmills or even
the wheel, none have survived even a few generations without art."*
—David Bayles and Ted Orland

As I said before, sometimes nothing else will do.

As You Begin

I'm honored when teachers ask me to sign their books or to visit their classrooms.
But the greatest satisfaction comes when a teacher takes one of my ideas and shapes
it to better meet the needs of her students. This book is simply a collection of ideas
organized around a launching framework. It is designed to be used as a starting
point for the many more ideas you'll have as a result of reading.

*"Ideas are like rabbits. You get a couple and learn how to handle
them, and pretty soon you have a dozen."*
—John Steinbeck

Let the breeding begin!

seeds

2

Poetry

A Match Made in Heaven

*"The crown of literature is poetry. It is its end and aim.
It is the sublimest activity of the human mind. It is the achievement
of beauty and delicacy. The writer of prose can
only step aside when the poet passes."*

—W. Somerset Maugham

ANSWER: Mirtie Spaw (1904–1991), my maternal grandmother

QUESTION: Why does Tanny love the rhyme and rhythm of language?

My grandmother loved poems, beautiful collections of rhyming words that told of her Appalachian heritage and of her faith. We would sit in the porch swing at her old white farmhouse and she would recite children's rhymes and sing traditional hymns to me. I loved the feel of her wrinkled hand in mine, the breeze in my face from the pace of the swing, and the sweet rhythmic words in my ears. Forty years later, I still remember my favorite:

"Come little leaves," said the Wind one day,
"Come o'er the meadows with me and play,
Put on your dresses of red and gold,
For summer is gone and the days grow cold."

—George Cooper, American poet

ANSWER: Mrs. Yates, my seventh-grade language arts teacher

QUESTION: Why does Tanny love to read and write poetry?

My seventh-grade teacher, Mrs. Yates, told me that she loved reading my poetry. She knew I was miserably shy, so she always praised me in writing or in a hushed voice. She commented in my writer's journal that I should consider submitting a particular one of my poems to a children's poetry magazine. One day she leaned over my shoulder during class and placed a postage stamp on my desk. She smiled at me and whispered, "Don't forget to send in that poem." With her stamp, I sent it in. It was published. Twenty-five dollars arrived in the mail. That money was worth nothing compared to the exhilaration of seeing myself in print.

Yes, this is a simplistic way of looking at it, I know. Of course there were many influences from my childhood that shaped my likes and dislikes, encouraged my talents and exaggerated my insecurities. But, like many kids, I was highly sensitive to the words and deeds of my teachers. One encouraging comment sent my confidence soaring. One sharp criticism injected me with lasting self-doubt.

I consider myself lucky. I have positive recollections of experiencing poetry as a child. As you might have noticed, these memories are tied directly to people in my life. Poetry is like that. It is the connecting of one soul to another: the poet to the reader, the teacher to the student, the student to the teacher, and the poet to self.

Do you want your students to love poetry? There's a lot you can do to make it happen. Teaching poetry is like matchmaking. If we want our students to fall in love with poetry, to get high from reading and writing it, we must create experiences where positive emotions run strong and judgment is absent. We must show the real side of ourselves, and be relaxed, open, and honest. Sometimes our stress levels run so high for so long that our students go for weeks without seeing this side of us. They'll remember these lessons where you didn't seem rushed and it was obvious that you loved what you were teaching. It's matchmaking: you know your students and poetry would be wonderful together, so you've just got to set them up on some instructional "dates."

Note: Maybe you don't love poetry yourself. Maybe positive poetry experiences never happened for you. That's okay. Perhaps you can use this launching sequence to do a little matchmaking for yourself!

Fig. 2-1 Granny Spaw's porch swing

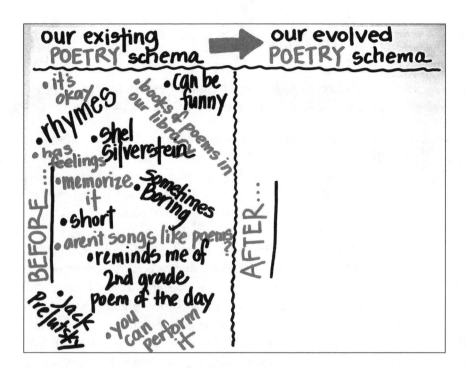

Fig. 2-2 Student think[i]
before the launching
sequence

I like to take a few minutes to see where my students stand when it comes to poetry. Using a large T-chart, I do a "One-Minute Schema Determiner" (see pages 33–36 in *Comprehension Connections: Bridges to Strategic Reading*, Heinemann, 2007). I jot down their thoughts, feelings, experiences, and opinions about poetry on one side of the T in a particular color. Days later, after teaching the lessons mentioned in this chapter, I revisit the chart. Using another color, I fill in the opposite side of the T with the new thinking my students have generated about the genre of poetry. It's good for me to know where the kids are coming from, and good for them to see how their thinking changes after learning and talking together.

Sometimes intermediate kids tell me how poetry bores them. And not just boys, either. There's nothing I hate to hear more. My fifteen-year-old daughter Brynne, who has been talking through this chapter with me as I write, says that sometimes poetry is taught in a way that is nothing but drudgery. Brynne says that kids need *poetry resuscitation* more than they need *poetry recitation*. I agree. For most kids, just one, no-strings-attached, honest experience with poetry can bring them into a relationship with this special genre. They say it's never too late to change your mind, and that's certainly true here. It's never too late for you to help change their minds about poetry . . . or more accurately, change their hearts. Let this launching sequence be your guide.

Launching Sequence: Poetry

Concrete Experience: The Poetry Jar

I begin by pulling the students up close and personal, expressing my complete fascination with this new genre we're about to explore. I typically begin with the stories I mentioned at the beginning of this chapter, stories about my grandmother Mirtie and my middle school teacher, Mrs. Yates. I explain that because these important people in my life loved poetry, I started feeling connected to this genre, too.

I know I can't go wrong by starting with story. In *Made to Stick* (Random House, 2007), Chip and Dan Heath teach us that a story is powerful in two important ways. It *simulates* and *inspires*. Stories allow our students to simulate real-life scenarios. When we tell a story, it gives our students ideas about possible ways to act and think, allowing them to reflect on ways they would act and think in a similar situation, sort of like a "life rehearsal." Stories are also inspirational to our students. They motivate our kids to do something with what they've heard, to take action. Through my stories, I want my students to imagine poetry as part of their lives and to consider poetry as part of their reading/writing diet.

In *Made to Stick*, the Heath brothers also discuss the concrete approach to thinking and learning, as mentioned earlier in this book. This poetry launch is a blend of "story" and "concrete."

The concrete object I use to launch this genre is a container of some kind. Mostly I use a glass jar, but I've used a Tupperware bowl, a Thermos®, and a Ziploc® bag on occasion.

I begin with a simple question: "How is poetry like a jar?" I jot this on a piece of chart paper or project it on a screen, depending upon what is available to me. I place the container in a prominent place, with the students up close around me. Asking the kids to turn and talk, to make this idea thinking-intensive, they are given time to explore the question. Some kids understand the metaphor right away, while others listen in and learn from their peers. No surprise here: their responses correlate directly with the kind of exposure and experience they've had with poetry in the past. I don't really comment here, or give affirmations. I just listen.

After a minute or two, I say to students, "Hold on to that thinking. We'll come back to it in a moment. If you are feeling unsure about how poetry can be like a jar, don't worry. Your thinking has had a good start and it will get deeper as we work and talk together. Right now I want to tell you about my dad. I will use this story to show you how poetry can be different from other genres, and how it can be like a jar. My dad is one of the most special people in my life and always has been. I can tell you about him in two ways: with my head, and with my heart."

Fig. 2-3 Kayla holds the poetry jar

With my head:

- My dad's name is Bob.
- He used to work at General Electric in Ohio but now he is retired and lives in Florida.
- My dad reads the newspaper every morning.
- He plays golf once a week.
- Every evening, Dad drinks Diet Coke® and eats potato chips.

With my heart:

- My dad has the kindest spirit of anyone I know.
- He speaks to everyone he meets.
- He treats everyone like a friend, even if he has never met the person before.
- Dad loves to take care of his family.
- I know he would do anything for me at any time.
- He loves me so much and has shown me in many ways all of my life.

By this time I am usually tearing up, but that makes the students all the more interested in the lesson. Hey, whatever it takes! I also want to be sensitive here, realizing that some of my students might not have a father like this in their lives. I tell them that they might be thinking of someone in their life who is like my dad is to me. Someone who cares about them. It could be a family member, a friend, a teacher or coach.

I ask, "What's the difference between using your head and using your heart?" The students turn to each other and talk, and usually there is no shortage of ideas. Here are some recent responses from a fourth-grade classroom in Lancaster, Ohio:

- You just give facts when you use your head. You don't really show your feelings.
- It's like nonfiction when you use your head.

- When you use your heart you aren't afraid to say how you really feel. You take risks.

- Your heart says what's really important.

Without saying anything further, I hold the poetry jar in front of me. I jot down the heartfelt thoughts I have about my dad on little slips of paper, reading each one aloud again for the students to hear. I drop the papers into the jar.

Then I ask the kids to think about the initial metaphor that I used to introduce the genre, poetry as a container. Sometimes I am guilty of "leading kids along," providing too much too fast when it comes to "solving" a metaphor. I'm trying to back off, give more wait time, and allow them ample time to make meaning for themselves. The outcome is always richer when the kids decipher the metaphor on their own, anyway.

So I present the container, and simply ask, "How is a poem like a jar? Talk to your friends and think it through." The wonderful thing about turning and talking like this is that the kids bursting with thoughts don't have to hold it in any longer. And their peers are a willing audience. For those who don't yet have a clue about this container business, they get a chance to listen and learn from others, in language they are likely to understand.

How is poetry like a jar?

- It holds thoughts and feelings so you can pass them on to somebody else. (grade 6)

- Poems hold my heart. (grade 2)

- Poems can spill out of you like water from a container. (grade 5)

- My feelings need a place to go so I can put them in a poem. (grade 4)

- A poem is a jar of secret stuff I think about. (grade 1)

- It is a jar of thinking. (kindergarten)

It's fulfilling to hear kids share this abstract, representational thinking . . . all derived from a simple, guided, concrete experience. But don't stop there. Now that your students get the idea about how this genre can be compared to an everyday object, allow them the opportunity to take their thinking even deeper with the following questions:

- How is writing poetry like giving blood?

- How is reading poetry like looking at an X-ray?

- How is experiencing poetry like being a daredevil?

In each case, present the students with an image to jump-start their thinking. Given time to think and talk, your students are sure to amaze themselves (and you!) as they explore this genre through a metaphorical lens. Here are some thought-provoking metaphors from my friend Mary's fifth-grade classroom:

GRETA: Poetry is a blender. The kitchen kind blends foods and a poem blends feelings.

ANSON: Poetry is a healing wound. When you have a physical and mental wound it is painful to have it reopen. When you write poetry, sometimes it is the same way. It can be painful to transfer your feeling into words.

SAMMIE: A snake twists and turns like a poem moves and grooves with feeling.

NICK: Poetry is like a vacuum cleaner. A vacuum sucks in dirt, and a poem sucks in you!

Here are a few quotations that encourage the same kind of thinking, comparing poets and poems to unlikely counterparts.

"Poets are like magicians, searching for magical phrases to pull rabbits out of people's souls."
—Terri Guillemets

"Poetry is ordinary language raised to the nth power. Poetry is boned with ideas, nerved and blooded with emotions, all held together by the delicate, tough skin of words."
—Paul Engle

"Poetry is a packsack of invisible keepsakes."
—Carl Sandburg

Even though this genre can be among the most abstract to interpret, it is among the easiest to make concrete. A concrete launch of poetry with students is one of those lessons I put in the "never fail" category, although maybe that category doesn't actually exist in instruction. I use this concrete experience to help kids notice and name the genre and to share my fondness for it with them.

Just doing a little matchmaking.

Noticing and Naming the Genre on Their Own

After the launching lesson, students are beginning to understand how this genre is special, how it holds our thoughts and feelings, how it connects with us not just as readers and writers, but as human beings. I want to be sure, however, that students have a chance to notice and name this genre on their own, discovering its unusual characteristics through observation and conversation. I was recently reminded how important this is when a fifth-grade girl told me she really hadn't read or written much poetry in her school career. We can't take it for granted that our students have a solid foundation in this genre.

I compile a small collection of random poems and distribute them to partners or small groups. Deliberately, I don't provide too much guidance for this exploration. I simply ask the kids to spend some time with this mini-collection of poetry and do some detective work. Of course they can read and enjoy the poems along the way, but the guiding question for this discovery is, "What do you notice about the genre of poetry?"

> *Note:* The small collection I provide for this exercise reminds me of the old wedding rhyme, *Something Old, Something New*. I include: something old, something new, something short, something long, something funny, something sad, something traditional, something that ignores the rules of capitalization and punctuation, something written in verses or stanzas, something written in a shape, etc.

My students seem to love this relaxed time for "uncovery." And I love to watch the process. Some groups choose to jot down their observations on sticky notes, while others enter information into a computer. However kids choose to track their thinking is fine with me as long as the process is steeped in conversation.

After a time, we come back together in whole group. A chart serves as the holder for our collective observations about what poetry can be and do. Ownership of the content of this chart runs strong. And all I had to do was give the kids a purpose and some time. Why is that sometimes so hard to do . . . when I know that the results are always so worth it?

Fig. 2-4 What students noticed during poetry "uncovery" time

Sensory Exercises: Poetry

Music Connection: Ella Fitzgerald (1917–1996)

Pearl Bailey once said that Ella Fitzgerald is simply the greatest singer of them all. And people all over the world agreed, earning her the nicknames "The First Lady of Song" and "The Queen of Scat." Ella won thirteen Grammy Awards and sold over 40 million albums.

Ella's voice is thought of as poetry in motion, with feeling taking over where convention leaves off. One form of vocal jazz that Ella perfected was scat singing. Ella left behind the lyrics on the page and sang nonsense words along to the rhythm. Many agree that trumpeter Louis Armstrong invented scat singing, but Ella Fitzgerald brought it to life, popularizing scat singing in the 1940s. I tell kids that when listening to Ella sing scat-style, you can almost tell when her singing moves from her head to her heart. Scat is like poetry, in that it gives a person a way to express herself without conventions getting in the way.

For a sensory experience that helps students make connections to the genre of poetry, introduce your students to Ella Fitzgerald. Listen to her ignore the confines of language while she scats.

Scat *is using your voice to sing with nonsense syllables or without words at all. The singer improvises, or creates melodies and rhythms without the limits of the conventions of language. Scat singers use their voices to play solos, just like a trumpet player or clarinetist might do.*

- ▪ "Blue Skies" (1958 stereo version) Ella Fitzgerald
- ▪ "How High the Moon" (live version, 1960 West Berlin) Ella Fitzgerald
- ▪ "Smooth Sailing" (1951 version) Ella Fitzgerald

Share photographs of her, show her album covers (available free at Google images or Bing), and read picture books about her life and style of music.

Fitzgerald, Ella. *A-Tisket, A-Tasket*. New York: Philomel, 2003.

Orgill, Roxanne. *Skit-Scat Raggedy Cat*. Somerville, MA: Candlewick, 2010 .

Pinkney, Andrea. *Ella Fitzgerald*. New York: Hyperion, 2002.

Weinstein, Muriel. *When Louis Armstrong Taught Me Scat*. San Francisco: Chronicle, 2008.

Share some of Ella's own words, and react together.

"I sing like I feel."

"The only thing better than singing is more singing."

"Just don't give up trying to do what you really want to do. Where there is love and inspiration, I don't think you can go wrong."

"It isn't where you came from; it's where you're going that counts."

Facilitate a conversation about the similarities between the genre of poetry and Ella's musical style, emphasizing how she made her own kind of music with her heart leading the way.

Art Connection: Robert Rauschenberg (1925–2008)

American artist Robert Rauschenberg is known for ignoring the conventional. He reshaped and redefined everything he touched. For decades, people have tried to categorize Rauschenberg's work: Is it painting or sculpture? Is it photography or printmaking? He said that his work filled in the gap between art and life.

Share Rauschenberg's work with your students. I especially like to share his *Combines* (1953–1964), where he took found objects and trash and merged them into his paintings, thus blurring the lines of the expected and traditional. He saw beauty in Coke bottles, soap dishes, and mirrors; he regarded them as everyday art that many people never notice.

Here are some pieces to look for:

- *Coca Cola Plan* (1958)
- *First Landing Jump* (1961)
- *Monogram* (1955–1959)
- *Pilgrim* (1950)
- *Satellite* (1955)
- *Untitled: Man with White Shoes* (1954)

There are many similarities between Robert Rauschenberg's creative approach and the genre of poetry. After taking some time to view some of the *Combines*, present these comments about Rauschenberg and his work. Ask your students: How was Rauschenberg like a poet? Here are some discussion starters.

- Rauschenberg took everyday items from real life and made you think about them in new ways. He gave new meaning to things.
- Rauschenberg didn't believe you had to stick to one way of doing things. When creating art, he broke the "rules" that others told him he should follow.
- Rauschenberg was an inventor.
- Rauschenberg improvised, making things up as he went along.
- Rauschenberg realized that not everyone would completely understand him.
- Rauschenberg always wanted to go beyond the limitations that others set for him.

Read to Learn More About the Genre

- Creech, Sharon. *Love That Dog*. Scholastic: New York, 2003.

This is a story about a boy named Jack and his dog, Sky. But it's really a story about words, how words give us a way to make relationships in life. And in the end, a poem saves the day, giving Jack the vehicle he needs to let his heart do the talking. In *Love That Dog*, readers learn so much about the genre of poetry, sometimes without even realizing it. Read aloud in the context of this genre launch, however, this heart-wrenching story can help you and your students grow your poetry schema.

Quotations About Poetry to Get Kids Talking

Find a couple of quotations from this collection that your students will enjoy thinking about. I tried to limit the number of quotes in this list, but there are just too many great ideas. I couldn't let go of a single one!

"I must study politics and war that my sons may have liberty to study mathematics and philosophy . . . in order to give their children a right to study painting, poetry and music."
—John Adams

"Poetry is the rhythmical creation of beauty in words."
—Edgar Allan Poe

"Breathe-in experience, breathe-out poetry."
—Muriel Rukeyser

"We don't read and write poetry because it's cute. We read and write poetry because we are members of the human race. And the human race is filled with passion. And medicine, law, business, engineering, these are noble pursuits and necessary to sustain life. But poetry, beauty, romance, love, these are what we stay alive for."
—Dead Poets Society

"Genuine poetry can communicate before it is understood."
—T. S. Eliot

"Poetry is all that is worth remembering in life."
—William Hazlitt

"Poetry is thoughts that breathe, and words that burn."
—Thomas Gray

"You can't write poetry on the computer."
—Quentin Tarantino

"Even when poetry has a meaning, as it usually has,
it may be inadvisable to draw it out . . . .
Perfect understanding will sometimes
almost extinguish pleasure."
—**A. E. Housman**

"Poetry is a deal of joy and pain and wonder,
with a dash of the dictionary."
—**Kahlil Gibran**

"Poetry is just the evidence of life.
If your life is burning well, poetry is just the ash."
—**Leonard Cohen**

"A poem begins as a lump in the throat, a sense of wrong,
a homesickness, a lovesickness."
—**Robert Frost**

"A poet is, before anything else, a person who is passionately
in love with language."
—**W. H. Auden**

"A poet's work is to name the unnameable, to point at frauds,
to take sides, start arguments, shape the world,
and stop it going to sleep."
—**Salman Rushdie**

"Poetry is a way of taking life by the throat."
—**Robert Frost**

"Poetry: the best words in the best order."
—**Samuel Taylor Coleridge**

"In poetry, you must love the words,
the ideas and the images and rhythms
with all your capacity to love anything at all."
—**Wallace Stevens**

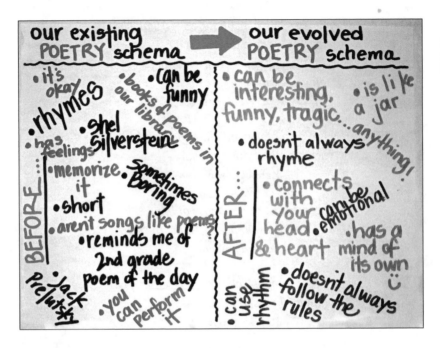

Fig. 2-5 Student thinking after the launching sequence

Time for Text: Poetry

Now that your students have a deeper understanding of what this genre is all about, investigate some of the amazing ideas that are available to guide your lesson design!

- Barton, Bob, and David Booth. 2003. *Poetry Goes to School.* Portland, ME: Stenhouse.

- Flynn, Nick, and Shirley McPhillips. 2000. *A Note Slipped Under the Door.* Portland, ME: Stenhouse.

- Heard, Georgia, and Lester Laminack. 2007. *Climb Inside a Poem.* Portsmouth, NH: Heinemann.

- Holbrook, Sara. 2005. *Practical Poetry.* Portsmouth, NH: Heinemann.

- Moore, Bill, and David Booth. 2003. *Poems, Please: Sharing Poetry with Children.* Portland, ME: Stenhouse.

- Janeczko, Paul. 2011. *Reading Poetry in the Middle Grades.* Portsmouth, NH: Heinemann.

- Pinnell, Gay Su, and Irene Fountas. 2003. *Sing a Song of Poetry.* Portsmouth, NH: Heinemann. *—gr k, 1, 2*

- Robb, Laura, and J. Patrick Lewis. 2007. *Poems for Teaching in the Content Areas.* New York: Scholastic.

ordered - Salinger, Michael, and Sara Holbrook. 2006. *Outspoken!* Portsmouth, NH: Heinemann.

- Tannenbaum, Judith. *Teeth, Wiggly as Earthquakes.* 2000. Portland, ME: Stenhouse. *primary*

seeds

3

Adventure and Fantasy

Beyond Realistic Fiction

*"I believe that imagination is stronger than knowledge.
That myth is more potent than history.
That dreams are more powerful than facts."*
—Robert Fulghum

A sandy-haired boy is perched at his desk. He gazes through the old classroom windowpanes and into the schoolyard. Though wide awake, he dreams that his desk has wheels and it carries him out of the classroom, down the deserted hallway, through the giant front doors, and out into the world. The boy's teacher later tells his mother that he has trouble paying attention. The next day his assigned seat is no longer beside a window.

A shy girl sits at a kidney-shaped table for a reading lesson. Steven is annoying her again today, with his incessant humming and pencil-tapping. The girl imagines a giant claw that swoops down and picks Steven up by his shirt collar, suspending him high enough above the reading group that she can no longer hear those distracting noises. She smiles to herself. At home that evening she writes a story about the claws in the ceiling of the school that only teachers know about.

Before you start to worry about these troubled youngsters, I must admit that the sandy-haired boy was my husband Miles and the shy girl was me. One recent Sunday morning we began recalling our elementary school days and how adventure and fantasy played a big part in our childhoods. For Miles, superheroes and futuristic vehicles filled his daydreams and his drawings. For me, talking animals and wild inventions showed up in my writing and in my backyard play. The genres of adventure and fantasy were part of our thought lives even before they were part of our reading lives.

The genres explored in this chapter are, as the brilliant developmental psychologist Alison Gopnik puts it, the "natural territory of childhood." Gopnik writes and speaks about how children use the fantastic, the unbelievable, not to escape reality, about which many adults worry, but instead to explore what might be. Dwelling in the realm of adventure, fantasy, and the otherwise outrageous allows children to think at high levels, creating syntheses of imagination and logic. As antithetical as it may initially sound, kids use a kind of scientific thinking while experiencing fantasy worlds, considering what *does* happen in the world with what *could* happen in the world. It's a study of similarities and differences, a testing of hypotheses and a formation of theories. And all of it is done safely within the imagination. Gopnik calls children the "R & D division of the human species." Her research at the University of California at Berkeley helps parents and educators understand why children love and need fantasy and imagination in their lives. To learn more, explore the many video interviews Gopnik has posted on the Web, and visit her website at www.alisongopnik.com.

These genres are important. They are not to be overshadowed by expository text, to be viewed as lesser or superfluous. Adventure and fantasy create a breeding ground in our brains where limitless possibilities, multiple solutions, and new hypotheses can grow. That and the fact that reading these genres is often incredibly pleasurable is a winning combination. The launching sequence to follow allows us to experience and discuss these sensational genres with our students, making some important discoveries as we go.

Launching Sequence

Concrete Experience: Prism

One of my treasured childhood belongings was a glass prism that a teacher gave to me. It was just a standard triangular prism, the kind included in many science kits. I had a toy box full of Barbies, stuffed animals, plastic dishes and more, but I loved gazing through that small piece of glass to see how the world was instantly transformed into a beautiful rainbow-filled wonderland. I would walk around the house, holding the prism right in front of my eyes, amazed at how it could still look like my living room, but at the same time look more interesting, more colorful, and more like a place in my imagination.

Regrettably, I've long since misplaced my favorite prism, but have acquired a few new ones from a teaching supply store. A wide selection also exists online, as you might expect, at a relatively low cost. Glass or acrylic, triangular or rectangular, what matters is that your students will be able to gaze into a world that seems magically different than their own.

With my students around me, I hold up a prism and explain that in 1666, Sir Isaac Newton conducted a series of experiments to prove that white light can be separated into different colors. He showed the world that light is split into colors that are bent by the prism. That's why, when we gaze through a prism, we see rainbows.

Fig. 3-1 A few of Tanny's prisms

I think aloud with this concrete object, just as I would with a piece of text.

I look around the classroom and say, "I'm in a classroom in Cincinnati. I see kids and books and computers and tables. There's really nothing unusual about where I am and what I see. I have a realistic view. But that's about to change!"

I take the four-inch prism from my pocket and hold it up for the students to see. Placing the prism before my eyes, I start to look around the room, and think aloud once again.

"Wow! Everything is different now. The things that are familiar to me, like tables, computers, and windows, are now coated in rainbows! I still recognize my surroundings, but it seems I'm in a fantasy world of color."

As you can imagine, the students can barely wait for a turn to look through the prism. Every time I launch these genres, I'm reminded of the power of concrete objects and how the engagement level rises as a result of their use.

With a prism at each table, students take turns gazing around the classroom and at each other. I hear exclamations like "cool!" "sweet!" and "no way!" The more light in the classroom, the more colorful the view. After everyone has had a chance to see the classroom in a new way, the students share their observations.

- "The prism made the room look magical."
- "It was like my eyes were on an adventure."
- "Everything looked real and unreal at the same time."

Show your students Joan Miro's *The Village of Prades* (1917) for a similar experience represented in visual art. Real, yet unreal.

After a few minutes I ask students to think about this experience metaphorically. "Did you know that there are genres in fiction that affect your thinking just like the prism affected your vision? Let's talk about it. What might I mean?" I provide support and guidance according to the grade level and sophistication of

Fig. 3-2 Third-graders in Rachel Ryba's class at Withamsville-Tobasco Elementary School listen as Tanny thinks aloud

my students' thinking. We talk through the comparison, listening to each other's thoughts and expanding our own. We talk about how fiction can be totally realistic, like looking around at your surroundings through your own eyes. But then again, fiction can be illusory, with fragments of reality showing up here and there, like looking through a prism. I name some of the genres on the fiction spectrum, pun intended: adventure, folktales, legends, fables, fantasy, and myth.

To boost understanding a bit, and make this experience even more concrete, I use a visual representation. With a black permanent marker, I've written the names of the focus genres on an assortment of prisms. I reveal them, clarifying the metaphor aloud again, using the labeled prisms as my props. I realize that many of my students do not know the differences between the subgenres in the fiction family, but now that I've named these genres through a concrete experience I can talk about what makes each subgenre unique.

I'll notice and name the characteristics frequently now, and have this concrete experience for reference. I can facilitate further thinking by asking questions and allowing time for talk. The concrete experience makes the abstract thinking possible.

Noticing and Naming the Genre on Their Own

To give your students a chance to explore these nonrealistic fictional genres with their peers, provide a bundle of representative texts for each small group. Find titles in your classroom or school library that fall into the focus genres of this chapter. You might include folktales, legends, fables, and myths, too. Facilitate the discussions with guiding statements. Sometimes I post these around the room on sticky chart paper, so the kids are surrounded by topics about which they can think and talk.

For primary students, pose thinking-starters like these:

- "Look at your group's bundle of books. How are they alike? How are they different?"
- "What do you see in the images or words that reminds you of real life?"
- "What do you see that seems like a dream or a fantasy, like looking through a prism?"

For intermediate students, consider these statements and questions to get conversation going:

- "Talk about what makes these selections fiction as opposed to another genre."

- "Would you classify each of these stories as realistic or unrealistic? What is your evidence?"

- "If you were to categorize these books or divide them into groups, how might you do it?"

- "What are some reasons why reading these fantastic, out-of-this-world genres can be good for our brains? What kind of thinking do you do when reading adventure and fantasy stories?"

And continue the thinking with prompts like these:

- "What fiction have you read that is just like real life? Tell me about it."

- "Let's find some examples of fiction in our classroom (or in the library) that are realistic stories."

- "What fictional stories have you read that are not very realistic? Maybe they are fantasy or adventure stories. What made them so unusual or out-of-this-world?"

- "Let's brainstorm some movies and video games that would fall into these genres. Why would you classify them this way?"

- "Do you prefer experiencing fiction that is true to life or fiction that takes you far from reality? Why?"

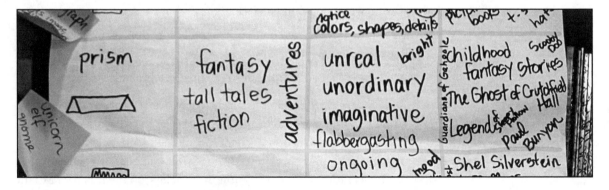

Fig. 3-3 The "adventure/fantasy" row on a genre chart, from Karen Kunkel's fifth-grade class at Summerside Elementary School

Sensory Exercises:
Adventure and Fantasy
Music Connection: Furniture Music

We've launched the focus genres with a concrete object. We've noticed and named these genres, comparing and characterizing, examining them from mostly a left-brained perspective. These genres reach way into right-brained thinking, too, with their newly imagined realities, fantastical settings, amazing characters, and unpredictable plots. Our focus genres for this chapter overflow with the writer's creativity, and at the same time light the fires of our own. The text pushes us into the stream of imagination.

So how can we give our students a taste of what this imaginative flow feels like?

It is a documented phenomenon that many people get their best ideas while showering, riding in a car, or taking a walk. Scientists tell us that instead of being intensely focused, our brains need to disengage so that imaginative ideas can rise to the surface.

Share with your students how creative thinkers, including writers, musicians, inventors, and mathematicians, uncover imaginative ideas:

While dreaming, the tune for "Yesterday" came to Paul McCartney, and the plot for *Misery* revealed itself to Stephen King.

While bathing, Greek mathematician Archimedes discovered the scientific principles of density and buoyancy.

While traveling by subway, minimalist composer Steve Reich gets unstuck and ideas for new compositions surface.

While traveling by bus, French mathematician Henri Poincaré conceived non-Euclidean geometry.

While playing *Pac-man*, yours truly got some great teaching ideas for this book!

Since sleeping, warm showers, and leisurely drives aren't likely options during the school day, how can we provide a few moments of relaxed creativity in our often overscheduled, fragmented instructional schedules? Our students' brains need some space so they can generate new thinking. Music is what's needed here! Music can be the backdrop for creation and imagination in our classrooms. It can relax and disengage our brains so new ideas can grow. Here are a couple of suggestions for "idea music" for your students.

Erik Satie (1866–1925)

Erik Satie was a French pianist and composer, an eccentric daydreamer who paid little attention to the musical norms of his day. Satie was progressive, artistic, and largely unappreciated until late in his life. In his compositions, he invented and intertwined themes, creating a playground for adventure and fantasy. It's no surprise that Satie's compositions are often classified as surrealistic and/or impressionistic. His music lets the thinker think and the dreamer dream . . . an ideal soundtrack for creativity and imagination. Erik Satie wanted his music to be like wallpaper: all around but not particularly paid attention to. In 1902, in fact, Satie purposely began playing what he called "furniture music," ambient music to fill a room, making it easier to relax.

Consider playing some of Satie's compositions when you and your students need to slow down, think out of the box, and create. Add some furniture music to your classroom while reading, while writing, while problem solving, visualizing, or brainstorming. Whether you listen to these pieces on YouTube or download them from iTunes, adding this atmospheric ingredient to your classroom will be a tribute to Satie himself.

Trois Gymnopédies (1888)
There are many piano and orchestral versions of these three works. Look for piano recordings by Michel Legrand or the well-known *Variations on a Theme by Erik Satie* by Blood, Sweat and Tears (1968).

Trois Gnossiennes (1893)
These three pieces have been used as furniture music in dozens of movies and commercials, including Martin Scorsese's *Hugo* (2011). Both *Coldplay* and Tori Amos have drawn attention to these pieces in recent years.

Today, furniture music is ubiquitous, unavoidable in nearly every store and restaurant. Erik Satie's desire for unobtrusive music has stood the test of time. Known better today as ambient or minimalist music, this musical genre has grown in popularity around the world. Innovator Brian Eno says that ambient music puts the listener into a different state of mind. Eno's *Ambient* album series hosts a collection of songs to try as well.

Fig. 3-4 Students listen to music during a lesson

One of my favorite ways to use Satie or Eno in the classroom is to use it to enhance text readings and visualizations. Play furniture music in the background while reading aloud from a well-known fantasy or adventure story. This is a great way to acquaint students with excerpts from exemplar texts from these genres. Let the music play softly as students conjure up ideas and images. Encourage doodling and drawing. Conclude with some conversation and a gallery walk to share images. Wrap it up by placing the book in the classroom library, since the combination of music and text will have piqued student interest.

Experiment with furniture music in different parts of the instructional day. The ultimate in creative ideas comes from relaxed thinkers, thinkers who are adventurous with rich fantasy lives.

Art Connection: Surrealism

Surrealism, a cultural movement that encompassed art, music, literature, film, and politics, emerged in the 1920s. Writer and poet André Breton (1896–1966) founded the movement. He believed that the unconscious, dreamlike state is the source of imaginative thinking, where thought-play is most likely to occur. The Surrealists encouraged creative acts to liberate the imagination. Surrealism is about the expression of thoughts, even when they are outside the realm of reason and reality, much like the focus genres of this chapter. Surrealists wanted people to liberate their imaginations and appreciate the element of surprise.

It's easy to see how this artistic style parallels the literary genres of adventure and fantasy: high creativity, deviation from the expected, and no limit to the imagination. Introduce your students to a few surrealists; view their work and talk about what you see.

- Salvador Dali: *The Persistence of Memory*, or *La Persistencia de la Memoria* (1931). The most well known of Dali's paintings, this work has a dreamlike quality, full of imagery.

- Meret Oppenheim: *Breakfast in Fur*, or *Le Déjeuner en fourrure* (1936). Oppenheim rose quickly to fame as a result of this imaginative piece: a teacup, saucer, and spoon covered in fur.

- René Magritte: *Personal Values*, or *Les valeurs personnelles* (1952). Unlike many other surrealists, Magritte took real-life objects and toyed with their proportion and relationship to each other. In *Personal Values*, he makes normal, everyday things seem strange.

- Max Ernst: *Ubu Imperator* (1923). There are so many ways to interpret this painting. It is an example of Ernst's fantastical creatures and wild creativity.

- Yves Tanguy: *Indefinite Divisibility* (1942). This work exemplifies Tanguy's nonrepresentational surrealism. It is abstract, mysterious, and just waiting for discussion.

And for the ultimate in synthesis, ask students to use their brain's wide lens, looking at this chapter's literature, music, and art all at once. How do the literary genres of Adventure and Fantasy overlap with Furniture Music and Surrealism? Sounds like a topic for a college syllabus, doesn't it? When kids are given the opportunity to experience these concepts, when they are able to notice and name what they see, and when they're given time to talk about their thinking, anything is possible!

Read to Learn More About These Genres:
Focus on Barbara Lehman

Perhaps I should entitle this section "*View* to Learn More About These Genres," as the featured books here are wordless, or nearly wordless. Can I say that Barbara Lehman is a genius? She is. I use her books practically everywhere I go, and for many different reasons: they are thinking-intensive, they are easy to view with clean lines and vivid colors, they encourage discussion, they instantly pull in the viewer, and, even though they're filled mainly with images, they tell tales of adventure and fantasy that give the imagination a workout.

At the time of this writing, Lehman has illustrated five wordless books. Her stories come from her own memories and experiences, and are mixed with her fantasies and dreams. Viewing and discussing Lehman's books can provide your students with a taste of fantasy and adventure as they experience these stories with each other. What is real? What is fantasy? How would the adventures of the characters extend if the book were to continue? There is plenty to talk about as these stories unfold through Lehman's imagination. Visit www.barbaralehmanbooks.com for greater insight into her work.

- *The Red Book* (2004). Find a red book, pick it up . . . anything can happen!
- *The Museum Trip* (2006). On a field trip, one child gets separated from the class. Adventure ensues.
- *Trainstop* (2008). On this train ride, it's hard to tell when reality stops and fantasy begins.
- *Rainstorm* (2009). Rainy day boredom? No excuses. There's always an adventure to be found if you'll just look.
- *The Secret Box* (2011). A tale of time-travel, treasure, and magic. Inspired by a real box of treasures from the early 1900s.

Quotations About Adventure and Fantasy to Get Kids Talking

"Adventure is worthwhile."
—Aristotle

"Fantasy is an exercise bicycle for the mind. It might not take you anywhere, but it tones up the muscles that can."
—Terry Pratchett

"It is only in adventure that some people succeed in knowing themselves—in finding themselves."
—André Gide

"I like nonsense. It wakes up the brain cells. Fantasy is a necessary ingredient in living."
—Dr. Seuss

"Adventure is worthwhile in itself."
—Amelia Earhart

"All acts performed in the world begin in the imagination."
—Barbara Grizzuti Harrison

"A work of art is above all an adventure of the mind."
—Eugene Lonesco

"The greatest form of finding out the truth is through fantasy."
—Joseph Fiennes

"Adventure is not outside man; it is within."
—George Eliot

"All cartoon characters and fables must be exaggeration, caricatures. It is the very nature of fantasy and fable."
—Walt Disney

"When you're safe at home you wish you were having an adventure; when you're having an adventure you wish you were safe at home."
—Thornton Wilder

Time for Text: Adventure and Fantasy

Here are a few titles that can provide instructional ideas as you move further into the study of adventure and fantasy.

- Calkins, Lucy, and Mary Ehrenworth. 2011. *A Quick Guide to Teaching Reading Through Fantasy Novels*, 5–8. Portsmouth, NH: Heinemann.
- Fulher, Carol J., and Maria Walther. 2007. *Literature Is Back: Using the Best Books for Teaching Readers and Writers Across Genres*. New York: Scholastic.
- Garner, Joan. 2006. *Wings of Fancy: Using Readers Theatre to Study Fantasy Genre*. Santa Barbara, CA: Libraries Unlimited.

Since professional books that specifically address adventure and fantasy are few and far between, you can find additional support in professional books that address fiction in general, like *The Genre Prompting Guide for Fiction* by Irene C. Fountas and Gay Sue Pinnell (Heinemann, 2012).

seeds

4

Historical Fiction

The Best of Both Worlds

*"The hardest part of my job is to figure out
how to weave together the fact and the fiction
so that you can't see the seam, how you sew them together."*

**—Tracy Chevalier, as interviewed on the Diane Rehm Show,
WAMU (NPR), January 14, 2010**

Dear Tracy,

That might be the hardest part of your job, but oh how you make it look easy! When I read your works of historical fiction, all six of them at the time of this writing, I find myself insatiably hungry to learn more about times, people, places, and things I had never considered before. You work your magic, staying true to history and filling the research gaps with your imagination. That's why I'm always waiting, waiting, waiting for your next book, checking your website for updates. You turn me into the kind of driven, curious learner that I want my students to be.

Gratefully,
Tanny

When I read . . .	I become curious about . . .
The Virgin Blue (1997)	16th-Century France, Calvinism
Girl with a Pearl Earring (1999)	Vermeer, the camera obscura
Falling Angels (2001)	Victorian funerary architecture, mourning etiquette
The Lady and the Unicorn (2003)	Medieval tapestries, symbolism in art
Burning Bright (2007)	Painter and poet William Blake, the French Revolution
Remarkable Creatures (2009)	Fossils, paleontologist Mary Anning

I've noticed something. My curiosity is piqued by historical fiction. History textbooks rarely do this for me; they inform me but after reading them I don't usually feel propelled to research or investigate on my own. In historical fiction, however, the story draws me in and keeps me, creating a curious drive to know more. I'm mesmerized by the tension between the real and the imagined, not exactly knowing which is which. I love the feeling.

Historical fiction lies on the continuum between fiction and nonfiction, and can be defined as an imaginative reconstructed present or past. The structure, for many readers, is familiar; the story inviting. This genre can be classified by place and period, and sometimes by character. Added features like maps, primary documents, lists of characters, and timelines make this genre even more compelling, and support comprehension along the way. Historical fiction is part of mainstream fiction, and has become increasingly popular.

I agree that this genre can present a challenge, with the reader having to determine what is true and what isn't, but I often witness it as a welcomed challenge, with the reader propelled to learn more on his/her own outside of the text. The perpetual questioning and inferring of the reader can't be denied, and are valuable beyond measure in deepening comprehension.

The icing on the cake, from a teacher's vantage point, is that historical fiction entices the reader while addressing content. It's the best of both worlds. It supports cross-curricular learning, that goal we are all trying to reach in our often fragmented and departmentalized school days. My daughter Blythe, a high school junior, says that if a topic in a textbook is too boring or difficult to comprehend, she can read about it in a piece of historical fiction and then it's more interesting and easier to understand. Blythe's comment makes me think about how underutilized this genre really is in my instructional repertoire.

I expect a lot from this genre. I want it to reveal itself on the continuum between fiction and nonfiction. I want it to be recognizable when heard or read, and enjoyed because of its story. I want it to make students curious about times, places, people, things, and events in the present and past, to spur them on to further reading and interesting research.

Consider the many types of historical fiction: time travel stories, fictionalized memoirs and histories, sagas, and tales of historical mysteries and romance, to name a few. These subgenres are popular because, as reader's advisor Joyce Saricks says, we understand history from the inside. Historical fiction has a unique way of pulling us in, of keeping us engaged and of revealing content simultaneously. And all we have to do is stay on for the ride.

Launching Sequence: Historical Fiction

Concrete Experience: Clothespin

I launch this genre by doing a bit of storytelling with an object that has been used for more than a century: the wooden clothespin. I give a clothespin to each student to hold while they listen, telling them that this object, along with the story I'm about to tell, will help them learn more about a new genre.

> Linda was born in 1942 in a quaint farmhouse in the green rolling hills of Kentucky. Like the eight brothers and sisters who came before her, she belonged to a family that was rich in love but not in money. As soon as she was big enough to walk, little Linda started following her mother around the house, learning how to do simple household chores while singing songs she learned at church. Everyone in the family worked hard, every day. Linda and her brothers and sisters still found time for fun, though, and often combined their chores with games and make-believe.
>
> Since they had no clothes dryer, the clean laundry had to be hung on a rope line that was stretched between two posts in the

backyard. There the fresh-smelling clothing and linens were attached to the line with one-piece, wooden clothespins, the kind invented in the 1850s. It was common to see Linda and her sisters and brothers sitting in the grass under the clotheslines, using the clothespins as dolls. They would take a pencil or a crayon and draw a face on the round wooden heads, then add some hair and clothes.

With the help of each child's hands and imagination, the clothespin dolls would run around in the grass, jump rope, dance, sing, and even kiss! Each day, the clothespin dolls became wooden friends to Linda and her siblings, until their mother called to say, "Time for lunch!"

At the conclusion of the story, I ask the students to turn and talk to each other, to share what they visualized while I told Linda's story. After bringing their attention back to me, I tell the students that part of the story is true.

"Linda is my mother. She was born in 1942 to a big family and had to do chores every day with her siblings. She did have to hang the clean laundry to dry in the backyard. But I'm not sure if she always made dolls out of the clothespins, and I don't know if they made the clothespins dance and sing. I do know that people back then did make toys out of everyday objects, so as I told the story about my mom, I used my imagination to fill in the gaps where I wasn't sure. I have even done some research on the Internet to learn more about clothespin dolls and to see some photographs of different kinds. My story mixes nonfiction, the parts that I know to be true, with fiction, the parts that my mind invents."

I take a clothespin and put it under the document camera. With a permanent marker, I write "historical fiction" along the longest part. I take a piece of fabric and write "nonfiction" on it, then take another piece of fabric and write "fiction." I love doing this part without talking at all; the students are typically very engaged and wondering what I'm up to. I ask the students what they think my actions mean, how these objects and my writing might add up to something that represents a new genre. Their responses are always interesting.

- "The pieces of clothes are going to go together." (grade 1)
- "You're showing us how to mix genres, Mrs. McGregor." (grade 3)
- "Sometimes when you're reading there is truth mixed with the author's imagination." (grade 7)

Still working with the clothespin and fabric under the document camera, I place the two pieces of fabric into the clothespin's narrow space. I position the clothespin so that the kids can see the label, historical fiction. Again, without explanation, I ask the kids to turn and talk about their new thinking.

If materials are available, of course it's a great idea to allow students to create their own historical fiction clothespin with fabric and markers. But if time doesn't allow or materials are scarce, the making of one model for the class is still a good way to launch new thinking.

This concrete experience helps me accomplish my goal: introduce kids to a genre, notice what makes it unique, and give it a name. The following ideas in this chapter take you and your students a bit farther down the path of understanding, on the way to experiencing the genre as a reader.

Fig. 4-2 Alex and Kevin put fiction and nonfiction together in a concrete way

Noticing and Naming the Genre on Their Own

An interesting way to give kids a chance to have conversation and make genre discoveries on their own requires just one simple resource: a collection of picture book jackets. You know, the book jackets you have in the cabinet, the ones you removed from the new books you got years ago—the book jackets that librarians usually have plenty of, stored in a closet somewhere. This experience works well after you've launched several genres, after students have noticed and named other genres and are familiar with their characteristics.

To begin, I bring my students up close to see a book jacket that I've chosen, or I might project the images and text for all to clearly see. I ask a student to join me and we think aloud together. Pointing out what I'm noticing from the text and illustrations, I share my hunch for what genre this book belongs to and invite my partner to do the same. We cite evidence from the front and back covers, the teaser blurb on the front inside flap, and from the author and illustrator bios on the back inside flap. Charting our thinking for the class to see and discuss is always an option when time allows. Students then turn and talk, discussing whether they support or question our conclusion.

After the think-aloud comes practice, so I gather a small collection of random book jackets for the class to work with. I make sure the genres that I've previously launched are represented, along with historical fiction, and throw in a couple of

Fig. 4-3 Gathering evidence from book jackets

new or unfamiliar genres to see what students can make of them. Providing partners with a book jacket for discovery and discussion makes for some interesting
eavesdropping for me!

> GUIDING QUESTIONS: To which genre does this book likely belong? What is your
> evidence? Draw upon your schema and mix it with the text and image
> clues you can find.

Here are some conclusions drawn by two fifth-graders when examining the
book jacket from *Brothers* by Yin and Chris Soentpiet (Philomel, 2006).

> "We think it is historical fiction because we read the book *Coolies.*
> Our evidence is it's the same author and the cover looks almost
> the same. *Coolies* was about Chinatown, which is a real place in
> San Francisco, and this looks like it will be there, too. And it was
> from like the 1800s, around there. But we think the story is from
> the author's imagination. Plus in the back flap it says the author is
> interested in Chinese people in American history."

We took a few minutes to discuss the supporting evidence. Image evidence cited included the Chinese characters on the front cover, the way the title is written vertically down the side, and the picture on the back cover that is from *Coolies*. Textual evidence from the front inside flap mentioned that *Brothers* is a follow-up to Soentpiet's *Coolies* and that it is a story about the first Chinese immigrants. The fact that we had "author schema" for this book helped us tremendously, plus the cover contained detailed images and quite a bit of text to consider, too.

Allow partners to examine several book jackets, discussing the possible genres represented, always citing evidence from text or images. Students can jot down their thinking on sticky notes and place the notes inside the jacket. Bring students together for a sharing circle at the end of this experience, asking them to bring their book jackets along. Create a chart, recording titles and inferred genres, along with evidence from images or text. As a side note, this is a great way to advertise books, with the investigation and discussion of book jackets acting as commercials for new reading options.

Sensory Exercises: Historical Fiction

Music Connection: *Halley Came to Jackson* by Mary Chapin Carpenter

I can't think of a better storyteller than Mary Chapin Carpenter. She is one of those singer/songwriters whose recordings cross the boundaries of musical genres and leave us full of emotion and new thinking. Chapin Carpenter has a degree in American Civilization, so it comes as no surprise that a thread of history is woven into so many of her songs. Mixed in with songs of love, life, and heartbreak are lyrics about everything from Hemingway's 1921 move to Paris to the Tiananmen Square Massacre in 1989.

Many of Chapin Carpenter's songs can be used as examples of historical fiction, but one song in particular is my favorite since an accompanying picture book is available. In *Halley Came to Jackson*, Mary Chapin Carpenter tells of the two Halley's Comet sightings in the twentieth century, and intertwines that information with a sweet story inspired by American writer Eudora Welty. (If read/listened to through the lens of Welty, these lyrics could easily find a place in the genre of memoir.) In the lyrics and picture book text alike, a father holds a baby while the comet zips across the sky in 1910. Illustrations and text give us an idea about what

Fig. 4-4 Sadie and Natalie read song lyrics together

it was like then to experience such a momentous event, one that only comes around every seventy-five or seventy-six years. And just like Halley's Comet, the story comes back around, decades later. But this time the baby has grown into an older woman who experiences the excitement and mystery of the comet from her own front porch. This 1986 sighting sends the woman back in time as she gazes at a scrapbook of her memories. Such a touching story. The few verses in the lyrics and story don't contain much text, but they overflow with feeling and spur curiosity. The song and book end with a line that makes us think about the next time Halley's Comet is predicted to visit, in 2061.

Experiencing songs with students is one of my favorite parts of teaching. No accompanying graphic organizers, no sticky notes, no list of questions to be answered. Just the music and lyrics and everyone together. Plus, songs are so easy to find on the Internet and so inexpensive; both long-term planning and last-minute lesson improvements can include an element of music that enriches our students. Some students prefer to listen with lyrics on hand, while others like to close their eyes as the music plays. Either way, enjoy *Halley Came to Jackson*, then listen in as your students turn and talk.

Enjoy the song once more, this time with the picture book as your guide. Just as we afford our students multiple readings with the same text, don't hesitate to offer multiple listenings with songs. Listen, turn and talk, then listen again. You and your students will notice so much more with a repeated play. The illustrations will fill in some of the background knowledge gaps, answering a few of the instant questions students will likely have. Make time for responding to the listening/viewing experience. Listen for insights, questions, and inferences, and then ask students to talk with a friend about the genre these lyrics might represent. Historical fiction? Memoir? Why or why not? I usually ask my students if they feel that more background knowledge would be helpful to deepen their comprehension.

You've listened together, read and viewed together, and talked together. There are so many ways to go from here. Facilitate discussion about how the marriage of fact with story is so incredibly interesting and how it can make you want to read more and do your own research. Visit Google Images for incredible photographs taken of Halley's Comet in 1910. I've witnessed the curiosity of kids as it leads them to find Eudora Welty's original story, to read and report back about Halley's Comet, and to discover that there is a Mark Twain connection in all of this, too. One song. One simple story with a bit of history tossed in. So much to enjoy. So much to learn.

Art Connection: Joseph Cornell (1903–1972)

Joseph Cornell was an American artist, known to be abstract, nostalgic, and very private. Like many artists, his interests and works varied over time. One way he expressed himself was through the creation of what has come to be known as "the Cornell box," not to be confused with the computer graphics test of the same name.

Cornell took found objects (I think he would have liked my launching lessons) and arranged them creatively in small boxes with glass fronts. Most of the works combined objects with various colors, textures, and shapes. Every time I see a shadow box, those deep picture frames that are quite common now, I think of Cornell and how he was way before his time. Items that we *can* see are grouped together to help us imagine what we *can't* see.

Just as an author of historical fiction mixes history with story, Joseph Cornell mixed real objects with the viewer's imagination. You can look at the real, the concrete objects that Cornell used, as a history of a time and place. When you view you begin to create in your mind what *isn't* there, thinking perhaps of why the objects are grouped together, what story they tell, or what memories they conjure. You, the viewer, are adding the story to the history that Cornell left behind.

Too abstract? Make it concrete. Revisit the wooden clothespin metaphor from the launching lesson of this chapter. Introduce your students to images of a couple of Cornell's boxes, and talk about his work, how he took everyday objects and arranged them in boxes so people could make them meaningful. Once again, show the historical fiction clothespin that you created previously. Talk about the significance. Then on a new clothespin, write "Cornell Box" on the long side with a permanent marker. Use two pieces of fabric (or paper) just like before, only this time label the first piece with "objects" and the second piece with "imagination." Allow your students time to turn and talk along the way, as you feel they need it.

Try thinking aloud for your students with a Cornell box of your choice. And then as you view images of Cornell boxes together, notice and name the objects. Allow time for students to talk in partnerships or small groups to imagine their stories. There are so many ways to go with this: talking about stories, writing stories, creating your own Cornell boxes of objects, etc.

Be sure to visit www.josephcornellbox.com to learn more about Cornell and his work. One section of the site, the Gallery, shows Cornell boxes created by elementary school students. You can even create, photograph, and submit your own boxes for posting. This site is for your viewing, not your students, as some images may not be appropriate for children. With artwork as with text, it is always best to preview, making the best decisions about content for your students. Capture the images you wish to share, or project only the pages with appropriate content.

Joseph Cornell, like a great writer, had original ideas and prompted us to have our own. And believe it or not, there is a song about Joseph and his ideas that you might share with your class. The song is titled *Ideas Are Like Stars*, written and recorded by none other than Mary Chapin Carpenter.

Read to Learn More About the Genre:
A (Nearly) Wordless Picture Book

■ Priceman, Marjorie. *Hot Air: The (Mostly) True Story of the First Hot-Air Balloon Ride*. New York: Atheneum, 2005.

This fun, creative book can't really make up its mind if it is wordless or not: onomatopoeias abound. But the text that is provided, especially the timeline at the end, merges history with story. Priceman's creative illustrations and presentation tell the true story of the Montgolfier brothers and their 1783 hot-air balloon, the *Aerostat Reveillon*. Its flight extended two miles and took eight minutes, with King Louis XVI and Queen Marie-Antoinette of France looking on. Believe me, if you aren't already familiar with what's fact and what's fiction in this story, you'll be surprised when you find out the truth! Did I mention the involvement of a sheep, a duck, and a rooster? I won't ruin it for you here, though; experience this book with your students for an authentic conversation about the mixture of history, story, and imagination.

Quotations About Historical Fiction to Get Kids Talking

After experiencing an introduction to the genre of historical fiction through concrete and sensory experiences, your students will likely have some thinking to share when connected to some of the quotations below. The reactions and opinions of my students to these quotations make me realize how powerful and necessary concrete and sensory experiences are, how they carry our thinking to deeper levels of understanding. Without some of the aforementioned experiences in this chapter, it is likely that many students would be ambivalent to these quotations, and I would feel as though the quotes were too difficult for my students to understand.

"Fiction is life with the dull bits left out.
—**Clive James**

"I find it fascinating to research the clues of some little known period and develop a story based on that."
—**Jean M. Auel**

"History is the present. That's why every generation writes it anew."
—**E. L. Doctorow**

"I can . . . create fictional characters to bring you close to the historical figures, and fall back on my imagination when the research runs out."
—**William Martin**

"Fiction reveals truths that reality obscures."
—**Ralph Waldo Emerson**

"Imagination and fiction make up more than three-quarters of our real life."
—**Simone Weil**

"Fiction is not a dream, nor is it guesswork. It is imagining based on facts, and the facts must be accurate or the work of imagining will not stand up."
—**Margaret Culkin Banning**

"At the heart of good history is a naughty little secret: good storytelling."
—**Stephen Schiff**

Time for Text: Realistic and Historical Fiction

The professional resources listed below can help you think more about this genre in action. But first I must mention a couple of unbelievable bibliographies of children's literature available to you, lists of titles that include historical fiction and the nonfiction that satisfies our students' curiosities. One bibliography is intended for grades K–2, and the other for grades 3–6, but these great stories transcend grade level when used for instruction. Both are included in the resource sections of these toolkits.

- Harvey, Stephanie , and Anne Goudvis. 2008. *The Primary Comprehension Toolkit: Language and Lessons for Active Literacy*. Portsmouth, NH: Heinemann.

- Harvey, Stephanie, and Anne Goudvis. 2005. *The Comprehension Toolkit: Language and Lessons for Active Literacy*. Portsmouth, NH: Heinemann.

Professional Resources

- Serafini, Frank, and Suzette Youngs. 2008. *More (Advanced) Lessons in Comprehension*. Portsmouth, NH: Heinemann.

- Zarian, Beth Bartleson. 2004. *Around the World with Historical Fiction and Folktales: Highly Recommended and Award-Winning Books, Grades K–8*. Lanham, MD: Scarecrow Press.

- Zarnoski, Myra. 2006. *Making Sense of History: Using High-Quality Literature and Hands-On Experiences to Build Content Knowledge*. New York: Scholastic.

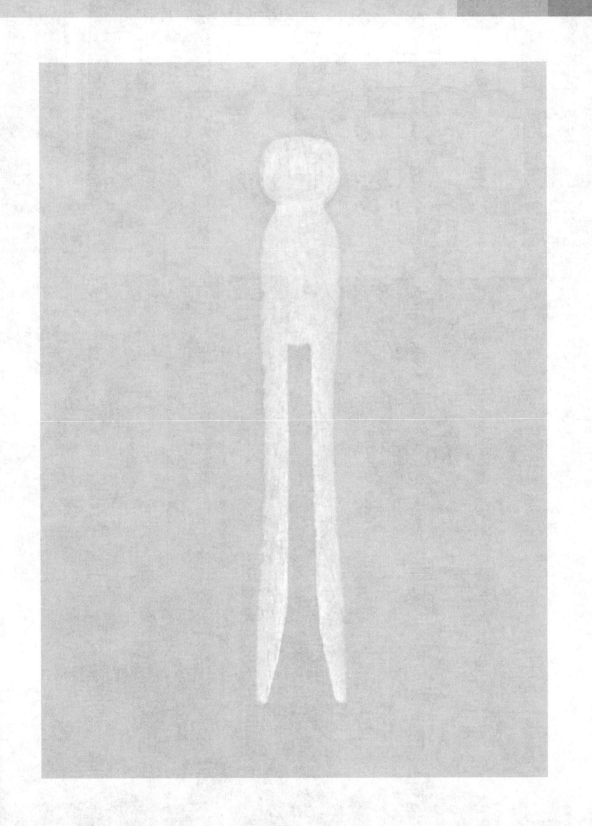

seeds

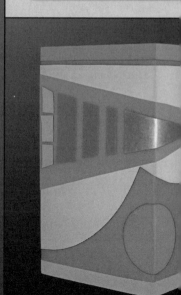

5

Drama

A Tough Act to Follow

"A play should give you something to think about.
When I see a play and understand it the first time,
then I know it can't be much good."

—T. S. Eliot

I was a first-grade teacher at the beginning of my career. What I lacked in experience I made up for in enthusiasm, and I could say the same for my students. I almost start to blush when recalling some of the crazy lesson ideas I tried that first year. On any given day one might smell fresh popcorn, see towers constructed from toilet paper tubes, and hear impromptu songs being sung. And everything for the greater instructional good, mind you. I knew that not everything worked for everyone. As a young teacher I discovered that there were dozens of ways to reach my students, and I wanted to try them all. Sometimes, an unexpected, unorthodox instructional idea worked like magic and the faces of my students lit up with sudden understanding. Other times, though, we all shared a heavy frustration—me wanting to find a way to make learning come to life, and the kids just waiting for me to figure it out. Sometimes I think, wow, I sure hope they turned out all right! They had to put up with me as a first-year teacher. But on the other hand, perhaps I was the most earnest, risk-taking kind of teacher I've ever been, with little fear of failure. In some ways, I wish I was that teacher again.

Looking back, there was a genre and accompanying instructional strategy that I had up my sleeve: drama. Reading it. Writing it. Acting it out. Role-playing. I didn't incorporate drama because I knew that research supported it as an essential genre to read and experience; I did it because it was fun. Everyone was engaged. And as a result, we learned. If the situation called for students to be more involved, more active, more present in their learning, we pushed in our chairs and became the content. In first grade we read simple Reader's Theater scripts and learned to read with prosody. We felt silly when the characters were silly, and sad when they were sad. We wrote our own math scripts as a class, showing how to tell time on an analog clock. We became the numbers and the hands, and learned to tell time by *being* the clock. Sometimes our reading and acting were part of formalized lesson plans, but other times they were as instantaneous and impromptu as can be.

After teaching hundreds of students at many grade levels, I have noticed that besides enjoying reading and acting out this genre, there are some unintentional benefits to reading and using drama in the classroom. I recognized these benefits with my first-graders back in 1989, and still see drama's positive influence reach across grade levels in many schools and situations. Here's what I observed: reading and acting out plays seemed to increase the level of collaboration and empathy among my students. I didn't see it at first. But the more this genre was present, the more I began to sense in my class an awareness of others' feelings, of why it is important to take turns, of how to work with a group of peers to solve a problem or create a product. Now here I am, almost a quarter of a century later, discovering that research finds the very same thing. So cool how that works out. Podzlony (2000) found that when children act out stories, their comprehension, language, and reading skills are strengthened, as compared with children who simply read the same stories. That same year, Verducci's research showed that because actors read and understand the emotions and behaviors of the other actors, they gain a greater understanding and empathy for those around them. Thalia Goldstein of Yale University, and Ellen Winner of Boston College and Harvard's Project Zero, state that empathy and theory of mind are crucial for everyday interactions and the ability to cooperate with others. The work of Goldstein and Winner (2012) suggests that both empathy and theory of mind are enhanced by role-playing.

Author/educator Roberta Mantione says, "Teachers see immediate classroom results when using drama. Students eagerly anticipate drama, showing us their motivation to be actively involved in text. During drama, they begin to demonstrate surprising insights that observers may have not seen before. After drama the class discussions become more engaging and to the point. Weeks later, students still make references to the characters and the book, and the important ideas and new words carry over into new conversations. Drama makes a significant impact on students" (from her foreword in *A Dramatic Approach to Reading Comprehension* by Lenore Blank Kelner and Rosalind M. Flynn).

Reading drama has merit in and of itself, too, even without active participation. Comprehending drama is a way for readers to deconstruct dialogue and human interaction, to understand story in a new way. When paired with Reader's Theater, acting, or simple role-playing, however, this genre becomes a powerful force in educating our emotion, as well as our intellect.

Launching Sequence: Drama

Concrete Experience: Puzzle Pieces

Fifth-grade teacher Karen Kunkel pieced together a small cardboard puzzle as her students looked on. We were clustered together in the small gathering place in Karen's classroom, talking to the kids about the genre of drama. Karen and I have taught many lessons together over the past decade, so teaming up comes naturally to us. I spoke about how this puzzle could be a metaphor for the genre of drama, with each piece representing a different element, about how the pieces fit together just right, and about how each part really needs the other parts in order to get the desired outcome.

There are many elements of drama, and when you begin to deconstruct this genre they become clear. We chose nine elements for our concrete launching lesson: character, plot, theme, dialogue/monologue, subgenre, audience, stagecraft, design, script. One of Karen's students mentioned how many of these elements show up in other genres. Another added that the elements of audience and script set this genre apart from the others. When kids begin to notice the genre, thinking about similarities and differences to other genres, we know our concrete model has done its job.

Consider using blank, cardboard puzzle pieces to talk about a play your students have experienced together. Assign an element to each piece and talk about it

as you put the puzzle together. As always, it's the thinking that we're after. We use the object to focus and engage, then layer on the metaphor to push our students' understanding to a deeper level.

Fig. 5-1 The genre of drama is like a puzzle

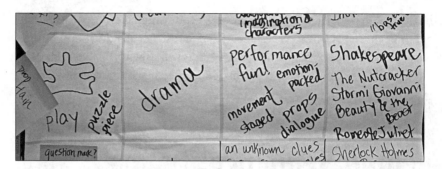

Fig. 5-2 Part of our class chart that holds our first thinking about the genre

Noticing and Naming the Genre on Their Own: Playwright William Green

One of the best things about writing this book has been talking with kids about genre. From many years of teaching, I already knew that kids, just like adults, have favorite genres. I knew that kids have specific genres they like to read and write. What has surprised me, however, is the level of genre expertise and passion that some students acquire at such an early age. Perhaps I just never noticed it before. Petra reads and writes informational text with ease. Tim reads poetry like there's no tomorrow, and what he writes touches my heart. And then there's William. William Green. To say that William has noticed and named the genre of drama doesn't even scratch the surface. He did that years ago! I can't *not* write about William in this chapter. To me, he is an example of the energy-giving power that a genre can generate in us when we connect to the reading and writing of it. William has found a genre where he can grow as a reader, writer, thinker, creator, and explorer. And we just need to get out of his way.

I first met William at a schoolwide literacy assembly. Summerside Elementary School in Cincinnati was celebrating Ohio's Right to Read Week, and I was honored to be the guest speaker. I read the picture book *Author* by Helen Lester and then talked to the K–5 students about the reading and writing connection. The highlight of the assembly had little to do with me, however. Principal Linda Austin pulled together a panel of student readers and writers who sat to my left as I spoke. They listened patiently, waiting for me to finish so they could share their reading and writing processes and a bit of advice for their classmates. These students spoke about persistence, stamina, and the importance of a good idea. As hundreds of their classmates looked on, this panel spoke the words that I thought only mature, seasoned readers and writers would know to share. I was humbled. And was reminded once again that if we give kids *time*, they show us *talent*.

Third-grader William Green spoke about a play that he has been working on for almost two years now. His folder bulged with the crinkled original copy of the script. As he spoke to the audience, I couldn't help but think about how the genre of drama had captured William, or he had captured it. Either way, it intrigued me. After the assembly I asked William's mom if I could have some time to talk to him about his work. So on a humid June morning I met William and his family at school. Just thinking back to this interview makes me smile.

Fig. 5-3 Playwright William Green

TM: Tell me about how it is to think about plays.

WG: Well, I started working on this play, *A Crazy Day*, in March of 2011 when I was in second grade. I never really know how I get ideas for plays; I never really know how I write them. It just comes to me. It just comes out and I start thinking and writing and it goes on and on. Sort of like writing a book, I think. A lot of late nights. The easy parts were (hesitates) everything. I can't think of anything that was very hard. But parts of it get me a little stressed, getting all of the details and trying to get it on stage just the way I imagined it. I try to get it as good as I can the first time, so I work hard at that so there's not too many mistakes I have to fix later.

TM: Where do you get ideas?

WG: Sometimes I get them from other books, TV shows, movies . . . and on long car rides I look out the window and see ideas in the clouds, like strange animals and characters. Then I try to get it down on paper if I have time. I have paper with me almost everywhere I go. Even in the car.

TM: To you, how is a play different than other stories you might read or write?

WG: It's not really very different in my eyes. When I read a book, if it is good, I can see it actually happening. Like on a stage. The only thing that slows me down is thinking, "Who is up next?" and "What are they going to say?" I wonder these things. I am interested in plays, and in first grade we had little plays we could act out, called Reader's Theater. I was Santa Claus in one play, and I think it got me interested. So by second grade I started writing my own. The most recent play I've read is *Pushing Up the Sky*, and I saw the same format in that play that I use in the plays I write.

TM: What advice do you have for other young playwrights?

WG: Although I have given advice to other kids in the past, I really don't want to give it. They should do what they want. The titles they want. The characters they want. The ideas they want. They don't need my advice. Maybe just remind them about punctuation and grammar, but that's all.

TM: I'm hoping this interview will appear in a chapter I'm writing about the genre of drama. Teachers will read it and think about your words. What would you like to say to them?

WG: I think teachers should always add in a couple of plays every now and then. And give kids lots of time to read and write and illustrate their own plays. Kids need to draw their characters so they can process the story in their minds.

TM: What does the future hold for you?

WG: I'm not really sure about being a writer when I get older. I've been practicing rapping a lot lately!

During the interview, William's mom sat silently, waiting to tell me a few things William failed to mention . . . like the plywood platform that he built with his dad in the garage, the set for the fight scene in *A Crazy Day*. Like how William asks for gift cards to Home Depot for his birthday, and how he has saved $150.00 so far for props and set materials. His grandma bought him his first hammer. William recently spent $37.63 to build a bridge. And he has started canvassing his neighborhood seeking investors for his drama company. William looks forward to a future production of *A Crazy Day* in a covered shelter owned by his aunt.

William has noticed this genre. He names it and calls it his own. A simple genre is the vehicle for his creativity, and is one of the places where his literacy grows.

In this book, many of the sections titled "Noticing and Naming the Genre on Their Own" contain ideas for releasing responsibility to students. In this section,

Fig. 5-4 William's scripts, sketches, and performance tickets

let's take a hint from William himself. What can teachers do to maximize the chances that kids will notice this genre, name it, and appreciate it? Make sure drama is represented in the genres explored and read in your classroom. Give kids time to read, write, and illustrate plays. In other words, introduce your students to drama and let them spend time together. Thanks for the reminder, William.

Sensory Exercises: Drama

Music Connection: Opera

When I was growing up, my family listened to many different kinds of music: pop, country, bluegrass, and gospel. But opera was not on the musical menu for my family, and even though we attended concerts, plays, and musicals every now and then, never did we visit the Cincinnati Opera, the second-oldest opera company in the United States, which was just a short drive away from our house. Fast-forward four decades. Here I am, with kids of my own, just learning about this musical genre and incorporating its power into my teaching.

I believe that our students deserve the right to be exposed to a diverse array of art and music, and if you've read *Comprehension Connections*, you already know that. Realizing that the average age of opera ticket-buyers and subscribers is around age fifty-eight, I realize we, as educators, can be part of creating a new generation of opera lovers (Daniel J. Wakin, "Met Backtracks on Drop in Average Audience Age," 17 February 2011, *New York Times*). After reading those statistics, my husband and I took our kids to see *Porgy and Bess* at Cincinnati's Music Hall, a good "first opera" for any age.

Think of opera as musical drama. Together, the vocalists and instrumentalists dramatize a story. Opera is, as K. F. E. Trahndorff coined it, a *Gesamtkunstwerk*: a fusion of music, poetry, visual art, and movement or dance. Opera synthesizes many forms of art, unifying them in the theater. When you're introducing your students to drama, exploring its uniqueness as a genre, then an introduction to opera is a natural extension. Don't be afraid if you've never listened to opera and don't know much about it. That will make the discoveries even richer because you'll be making them alongside your kids. Listen, read, and react together. Identify similarities and differences between the genre of drama and the art form of opera. There's nothing like experiencing something new with your students.

There are many resources that introduce kids to opera. Videos and recordings can be easily accessed via the Internet. YouTube clips of Jackie Evancho, and other young singers, allow kids to hear opera songs performed by someone their own age. Since video allows you to view the sets and see the facial expressions of the singers, DVDs offer a more complete experience for the novice, the next best thing to actually attending a live performance.

Free teacher resources, with elementary students as the intended audience, are available from the Metropolitan Opera's website. Visit www.metoperafamily.org and click on the Education link. There you'll find educator guides for dozens of operas, along with audio clips and story synopses. Many other opera houses have websites with free educational resources posted as well, like the Kentucky Opera at www.kyopera.org.

One of my favorite resources is a collection of fourteen well-known arias (expressive melodies, each performed by one person) that are recorded by opera stars. This CD, titled *The World's Very Best Opera for Kids in English*, brings together operas from many eras and composers, and even includes a few singalong tracks for those brave enough to try opera karaoke! The ISBN is 189450252-3, and a teacher's guide is available.

Operatic tenor Luciano Pavarotti wrote the introduction to a wonderful opera storybook called *Sing Me a Story*, written by Jane Rosenberg. The exciting stories of fifteen operas are told alongside illustrations of main characters and key scenes. Rosenberg's words and pictures arouse interest in the opera and encourage visualization as the stories unfold. These stories would be good to use as you prepare your students for the opera experience. Each opera is represented in just a few pages; so listening to an aria from each along with the read-aloud would be ideal.

Actor Richard Gere has been quoted as saying, "People's reaction to opera the first time they hear it is extreme. They either love it or they hate it. If they love it, they will always love it. If they don't they may learn to love it, but it will never become part of their soul."

I will admit, I didn't love opera the first time I heard it. Maybe that's because I was into young adulthood before my first true exposure. Gere may be right; opera may never become part of my soul. I appreciate it, though, and find pleasure in listening to it and thinking about the stories. I want my students to experience this musical genre and to realize how it is yet another way to share a meaningful story with others. I want them to have the knowledge they need to begin seeing how literature, music, and art intersect, and how textual genres are echoed in many types of human expression.

Although patronage to the opera has decreased in recent decades, with families choosing to be entertained through movies, downloaded music, television, and the Internet, we can do our part to share this theatrical genre with the next generation, and support the teaching of drama at the same time.

Art Connection: Living Pictures

For centuries, actors and artists have collaborated to inspire, inform, and entertain. Creating a living picture, or more accurately, a tableau vivant, is a way to merge the art of the stage with painting or photography. A living picture is a person, or group of people, who poses without speaking or moving. Historically, living pictures have been used to recreate famous paintings on stage, to contribute to the fanfare of royal ceremonies or to the meaningfulness of religious services. Sometimes a series of these staged poses would be sequenced in order to "tell" a story, like the nativity plays in Victorian England. When radio and film came along, the popularity of living pictures declined.

Provide a collection of portraits, either photographs or reproductions of paintings. An art teacher might be able to help here, or simply print pictures from Google images. Let each student study a portrait of their choice, noticing body placement, gestures, and expressions. Then students recreate this artistic pose as closely as possible. There are so many ways to go with this: playing guessing games where students match the pose to the painting, making inferences about the character's feelings and situation, etc. Point out that actors must recreate poses when bringing drama to life, and details matter.

Ask an art educator to suggest some portraits for this lesson, or try my recommendations below. I like to pair up students with each portrait so they can provide feedback to each other. For group tableaux, see books listed below.

- *American Gothic* by Grant Wood
- *Captain Cold or Ut-ha-wah* by William John Wilgus
- *General William Tecumseh Sherman* by George Peter Alexander Healy
- *Girl with a Pearl Earring* by Johannes Vermeer
- *Harriet Beecher Stowe* by Alanson Fisher
- *Joan of Arc* by Dante Gabriel Rossetti
- *Migrant Mother* by Dorothea Lange
- *Mona Lisa* by Leonardo da Vinci
- *The Scream* by Edvard Munch
- *Two Angels* detail painting by Raphael
- *Whistler's Mother* by James McNeill Whistler
- *William Buckland* by Charles Willson Peale
- 1941 photograph of Winston Churchill, taken by Yousuf Karsh

- 1942 photograph of Salvador Dali, taken by Philippe Halsman
- 1969 photograph of Buzz Aldrin, taken by Neil Armstrong

If your students enjoy, and they will, the combination of art, drama, and movement, you must investigate these two books. Both show how to use tableaux across the school day, with various genres and for various purposes.

- *Reading IS Seeing: Learning to Visualize Scenes, Characters, Ideas, and Text Worlds to Improve Comprehension and Reflective Reading* by Jeffrey D. Wilhelm (Scholastic, 2004). This book contains more ideas than you can believe. I tried to tab the ones I wanted to try and had to stop since I was tabbing every page. There are several kinds of tableau lessons here, including using tableaux with narrative texts, idea tableaux, and tableau sketches.

- *Texts and Lessons for Content-Area Reading* by Harvey "Smokey" Daniels and Nancy Steineke (Heinemann, 2011). This book is a secondary teacher's dream come true! It holds dozens of relevant informational articles and pairs them with engaging instructional ideas to be used across subject areas. If you teach elementary, the lessons can easily be adapted; just use appropriate text. Daniels and Steineke explain how to use tableaux in the content areas, providing step-by-step instructions, plus variations like speaking statues and action statues. I have had the privilege of participating in this strategy with Nancy and Smokey at the lead. I can tell you exactly what I learned that day about the Pueblo Revolt. This approach to content is unforgettable!

Read to Learn More About the Genre:
Reader's Theater

I always question myself when spelling Reader's Theater. Or is it Readers' Theater, Reader's Theatre, or Readers' Theatre? No matter how you spell it, Reader's Theater is a great example of the power of drama. Let me define the term for new teachers or those who might be unfamiliar with this concept.

Reader's Theater engages students with text through active involvement. It merges reading, listening, and speaking in an authentic, experiential way. Readers practice and perform a script for an audience. These repeated readings lead to greater reading fluency, but that's not the only benefit. Collaboration is the name of the game here. Some of the most productive small-group work I've ever witnessed happened during rehearsals for Reader's Theater, self-directed by students. In reading scripts aloud, the focus is on prosody, with facial expression and gestures only adding to the fun. Memorization is not necessary, and neither are sets or props.

Not only are Reader's Theater scripts more available than ever, the quality of scripts has improved through the years. Countless scripts are posted at no cost on the Internet, and inexpensive books of scripts are available for purchase. Here are a few resources to investigate:

- www.aaronshep.com (find free scripts and loads of resources)
- The Aaron Shepard Series: *Readers on Stage, Folktales on Stage, Stories on Stage* (Shepard Publications)
- www.scriptsforschools.com
- www.storycart.com

Reader's Theater has been around for a long time, and is used in more ways than you can count. You'll just have to find (or create) a way that works for you and your students.

Quotations About Drama to Get Kids Talking

"Drama is life with the dull bits cut out."
—Alfred Hitchcock

"Drama read to oneself is never drama at its best, and is not even drama as it should be."
—George P. Baker

"I made mistakes in drama. I thought drama was when actors cried. But drama is when the audience cries."
—Frank Capra

"One of the greatest things drama can do, at its best, is to redefine the words we use every day such as love, home, family, loyalty and envy."
—Ben Kingsley

"The drama is a great revealer of life."
—George P. Baker

*"The office of drama is to exercise, possibly to exhaust,
human emotions. The purpose of comedy is to tickle those emotions
into an expression of light relief; of tragedy, to wound them
and bring the relief of tears. Disgust and terror
are the other points of the compass."*
—Laurence Olivier

Time for Text: Drama

Now that you've whet the appetites of your students, delve more deeply into drama. These books will teach you how to use drama as a tool to deepen comprehension, develop confidence, and inspire creativity in your students.

- Freeman, Judy. 2007. *Once Upon a Time: Using Storytelling, Creative Drama, and Reader's Theater with Children in Grades PreK–6.* Santa Barbara, CA: Libraries Unlimited.

- Kelner, Lenore Blank, and Rosalind M. Flynn. 2006. *A Dramatic Approach to Reading Comprehension.* Portsmouth, NH: Heinemann.

- Miller, Carole, and Juliana Saxton. 2004. *Into the Story: Language in Action Through Drama.* Portsmouth, NH: Heinemann.

- Swartz, Larry. 2002. *The New Drama Themes,* 3rd edition. Markham, ON: Pembroke.

6

Image Reading

Stop, Look, and Learn

*"Of all of our inventions for mass communication, pictures still
speak the most universally understood language."*
—Walt Disney

In 1983, my friends and I went to the Cassinelli Square Cinemas to see
National Lampoon's *Vacation*, one of the silliest movies I have ever seen.
The Grand Canyon scene is my favorite part. After a long, tiring car trip
with the family, Chevy Chase pulls up to the rim of the canyon and everyone piles
out. Chevy puts his arm around his wife's shoulders, gazes out at the canyon for
exactly two seconds while bobbing his head up and down, then sprints back to the
car. He has seen enough. I guess the majesty of the Grand Canyon just wasn't
enough to keep Chevy's attention.

Sadly, this scene is reenacted almost every day. People of all ages stop to view a
painting or sculpture for just two seconds. Or look at a picture on the Internet or a
photograph in a book and quickly move on. No thinking. No real seeing. It's a bit
like speed reading. You might be lucky enough to get the gist, but the richness and
complexity is lost to you. Just as we teach comprehension strategies to encourage
deep reading, there are visual thinking strategies to be discovered that enable deep
seeing. Researcher Anne Berthoff says, "Students who learn to look and look again
are discovering their powers."

In conversations with teachers I sense some doubt that image reading is rigorous literacy. Let me pull up my soapbox. Image reading *is* real reading. Just because
your students are processing visually doesn't mean it's not worthwhile, not academic, not rigorous. It is actually *more* of all of those things. Because your students

have been reading this way since they were babies, they have some proficiency already. We forget that they were reading long before their names were ever even on our class lists. They've been reading body language, facial expressions, photographs, logos, and more since the day they started to see. So rest assured, image reading is not "literacy lite." If you see it, and you think about it, you are reading it!

Authors and researchers have written thousands of books and articles about creating and maintaining a print-rich environment . . . but let's not forget the importance of an image-rich environment. There's deep thinking to be had and heard when we immerse ourselves in nonlinguistic representation. As researcher Lawrence R. Sipe reminds us, the interpretation of images allows for ambiguity and multiple interpretations, which result in higher levels of thinking (2008).

Launching Sequence: Image Reading

Concrete Experience: Cereal Boxes

Jim Trelease, the author of *The Read-Aloud Handbook*, is right. The breakfast table is an ideal place for a kid to do some reading. Growing up in the 1970s, I practiced image reading with cereal boxes nearly every morning at the kitchen table. Boxes of *Apple Jacks*, *Raisin Bran*, and *Honeycomb* (still my all-time favorites) gave me a lot to think about as I started my day. Not quite metacognitive about it until my teen years, I still noticed font style, color, graphics, and design. I knew what I liked and what didn't appeal to me. Even though I was young, I realized that the designers of these packages had kids like me in mind. There was text to be processed as well, but I didn't decode in isolation. The images and design helped me deepen my thinking. These days, many of our students eat breakfast on the run or at school. But using cereal boxes as a concrete way to experience image reading still works, just like it did for me so many years ago.

First, I bring my students together up close. I take a box of one of my favorite cereals and think aloud. Here's how it went when I recently taught this launching lesson with a group of third-graders in Cincinnati.

"Hmm. Here's a box of bite-size Frosted Mini-Wheats, straight from my pantry. When I sit down at the kitchen table to eat a bowl of cereal, I usually set the box right beside the bowl so I can look at the images and read the text. I started doing this when I was a little girl, and thought it was so much fun. Pretend with me for a moment that I'm at home in my kitchen enjoying a bowl of Frosted Mini-Wheats. Here's what might be going on inside my head while I read the box."

I notice things like these:

- The Kellogg's® company used a bright color to get my attention at the grocery store.
- They used a photograph on the bottom left corner of the box to show how delicious the cereal looks.
- You can see the healthy whole-grain side of each piece and the yummy, sweetened side. I won't feel so guilty eating this cereal as I do when I eat a more heavily sweetened cereal.
- There aren't any cartoons or attention-getters for kids on the front. I wonder if more adults than kids like this product?
- The font looks sort of playful, not too serious.

My observations give kids examples of how to get started with their own thinking, what kinds of things to start noticing, and how to talk about it with each other. Then I turn the box around to examine the back. With a document camera, I project a photograph of the back of the box onto the screen. I ask the kids to take a look and think about what they notice. The back of the box is a lot different than the front, so I give them a few minutes to read the images and to talk to each other. The students make some interesting comments while image reading:

- The back of the box looks more kid-friendly.
- It even has a game to play.
- The little Frosted Mini-Wheats have faces.
- They used different colors on the back than on the front. I wonder why?
- There are more pictures to read than words to read.

Next step: unveil a variety of cereal boxes. Bring in a few from home, buy a couple that are interesting, and collect some from kids in advance. That's about all you have to do to get everyone engaged! There's just something about linking the everyday object from home to a lesson at school that makes kids automatically interested. In my experience, right away students have so much to say about cereal boxes that I grant them a few minutes to look and talk. They want to tell someone about their cereal likes and dislikes, about the toys available inside, etc. I usually do this with kids talking informally together, not in a guided discussion. They have a lot to say, but they are satisfied to tell each other; they don't necessarily need to tell me.

Next, I allow partners to choose a box to read. All they need is a cereal box and some time to think and talk. Sometimes students jot down observations on small sticky note strips to tag part of the design (image or text) that triggers new thinking.

When kids come back together, they bring the boxes to the sharing circle. I guide the session with questions like:

- What did you notice about the colors?
- Why did the designers of the box use the images they chose?
- Have you ever noticed any of these things before today?
- What are you wondering as a result of your time spent image reading today?

This launching lesson is an intentional way to guide your students to deeper image reading. They can also greatly benefit from incidental opportunities for noticing and thinking about images. Consider these simple additions to your routine.

- Create an "image of the week" corner. At the beginning of each week, display a new photograph, reproduction, advertisement, cartoon, etc. Simply post a question beside the image to get kids thinking. Questions might include: What do you notice? Is somebody trying to tell you something? What feeling(s) do you get from reading this image? What new thinking does this image generate for you?

- First thing in the morning, or at the beginning of a bell or class period, project an image on your screen or whiteboard. You can quickly find images that connect to previous or upcoming content. Provide the name of the artist, or list the publication or website from which the image was retrieved. In this way you can expose your students to thought-provoking images they might not otherwise view. Attach a thinking stem . . . or not. It's sometimes enough to provide the thinking stimulus and just see what happens.

- After viewing and talking, ask students to create their own title for a featured image. Encourage kids to notice colors, lines, shapes, mood, small details, etc. This is synthesis in action! You can even cover parts of the image to help students look more closely at an isolated section.

- Distribute laminated images to take home for "homework." Assignment: get a family member or friend's opinion about this image. Ask them to finish this statement: "What I notice about this image is . . . ." Students jot thoughts on sticky notes and adhere them to the back of the image, ready to share the collected thinking in class.

■ See chapter 14 in *Comprehension Going Forward* (Heinemann, 2011) for even more ideas to add to your image reading repertoire.

In his 21st Century Fluency Project, author Ian Jukes says that media fluency involves "the ability to look analytically at any communication media to interpret the real message, how the message is being used to shape thinking, and evaluate the efficacy of the message" (www.committedsardine.net). In a simple way, this initial experience with cereal boxes launches your students into that world of media fluency. Because you are devoting time to the viewing and interpretation of images, you are conveying that this sort of reading is, indeed, valuable.

A fun, free resource to help kids think critically about commercial images, noncommercial images, and editorial content is www.admongo.gov. The Federal Trade Commission created this web-based site to teach students through game-play how to interpret the images around them. It's my recommendation for independent exploration of this topic.

Noticing and Naming the Genre on Their Own: Twenty-Four-Hour Image Collection

Images are everywhere. They inform us, excite us, challenge us, annoy us. We can't escape their presence. Whether we're on the road, at the mall, on the Internet, or watching television, we are likely to be viewing and processing more images than we realize. It is estimated that people are exposed to about 5,000 images every twenty-four hours. Our students have really never lived any differently. They are

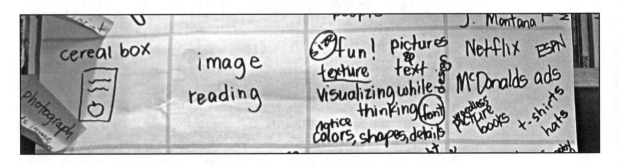

Fig. 6-1 A genre chart captures our thinking about image reading

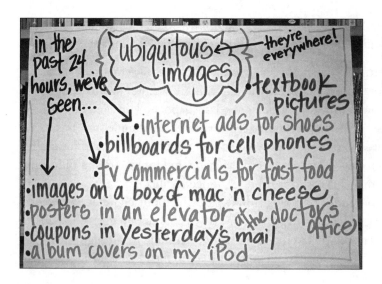

Fig. 6-2 Just a few of the images kids encounter in their everyday lives

used to images flooding their viewing spaces. *New York Times* reporter Louise Story writes that "blank spaces" should be added to the endangered list.

By noticing and naming the images that surround them, students can realize how ubiquitous the image is in their lives. Ask students to keep a journal or record of the number and kinds of images they encounter in a twenty-four-hour period.

When students bring their lists to share, create a quick class chart to record the multiple kinds of images that surround us daily. Post the list in an accessible space so kids can add to it later. Former Librarian of the U.S. Congress Daniel Boorstin said, "The force of the advertising word and image dwarfs the power of other literature." Your students will begin to realize the power of the image as you proceed through this launching sequence.

Sensory Exercises: Image Reading

Music Connection: "Vincent" by Don McLean

Some of the strongest images I've ever "seen" have come to me while listening to music. Science backs me up on this. Music influences the way you feel, which influences the way you think. Advertisers know this, movie-makers know this, church leaders know this, and dentists know this. Music has an effect on learning, memory, productivity, and mood. While listening to music, the release of enzymes in our brain can cause us to "see" images clearly, images that are original to our own thinking.

I first heard "Vincent" by Don McLean when I was at the department store with my mother in 1971. I was trailing right behind her while she shopped for items for our family, but in my mind I was a million miles away. I was a little kid who had never heard of Vincent van Gogh and had probably never seen even one painting he'd created. But the images I conjured up in my mind while listening to the lyrics and music were clear and sad. I wanted to hear the song again so I could get those images back. Lucky for me, "Vincent" got a lot of radio play in the early 1970s, so I could make a mental movie of this song again and again.

Try it out with your students. Play Don McLean's "Vincent" while students listen. Ask them to pay attention to the images they "see" while the music plays. They can share these images with the class or turn and talk with each other. Be sure to tell them what you see as well. Mention colors, landscapes, shapes, and people you see.

Fig. 6-3 For Natalie and Brenden, the music makes the lesson more engaging

After this initial experience with creating mental images, begin to construct some background knowledge together. Tell the students that a musician named Don McLean wrote this song. Years ago, McLean read a book about artist Vincent van Gogh and was very touched by van Gogh's life story. To pay tribute to the painter and his work, McLean wrote the song "Vincent" in 1971. Within a year it became a huge hit in Great Britain and the United States. Josh Groban, NOFX, Garth Brooks, Julio Iglesias, and many others have since covered it.

"I think that, in general, the most important thing educators can do to develop children's visual literacy is to adopt an inquiring stance themselves in relation to picture books" (Sipe 2008). Huddle up and read one or more of these interesting picture books about van Gogh's life and work. My personal pick is *van Gogh and the Sunflowers*, written and illustrated by Laurence Anholt. Of course you should decide how much time is appropriate to spend in discussion about the end of van Gogh's life. As always, you know your students and your community, and can design your instruction in response.

Anholt, Laurence. *van Gogh and the Sunflowers*. Hauppauge, NY: Barron's, 1994.

Holub, Joan. *Vincent van Gogh: Sunflowers and Swirly Stars*. New York: Grosset & Dunlap, 2001.

Metropolitan Museum of Art. *Vincent's Colors*. San Francisco: Chronicle Books, 2005.

Venezia, Mike. *van Gogh*. Chicago: Children's Press, 1988.

The perfect marriage of image and song is right at your fingertips. Mississippi artist Anthony DiFatta created a video that uses McLean's voice and van Gogh's paintings to allow the viewer to do some musically inspired image reading and see a wonderful representation of the body of van Gogh's work at the same time. I am moved each time I watch this YouTube video. View it with your students to "read" van Gogh in a musical, meaningful way.

http://bit.ly/RT2o73

For more of this powerful viewing/listening experience, enjoy William Lach's *Can You Hear It?* (Abrams, 2006), from the Metropolitan Museum of Art *Can You Find It?* series. Great art and music are paired up and at your fingertips in this book/CD set.

And with so many easy-to-use, inexpensive digital media websites out there, your students can create their own viewing/listening experiences. Try www.animoto.com, www.glogster.com, and www.voicethread.com.

After viewing van Gogh's work, listening to one or more of the recordings of "Vincent," and reading about his life, set aside some time for your students to react to Vincent himself. I like to play "Vincent" in the background while kids discuss their interpretations of van Gogh's own words. Here are a few of his better-known quotations.

- "I see drawings and pictures in the poorest of huts and the dirtiest of corners."
- "A good picture is equivalent to a good deed."
- "I dream of painting, and then I paint my dream."
- "I often think that the night is more alive and more richly colored than the day."
- "I put my heart and my soul into my work, and have lost my mind in the process."
- "I wish they would only take me as I am."

Art Connection: Ken Zylla

I discovered artist Ken Zylla quite by accident. After moving across town a couple of years ago, mail addressed to the previous residents kept showing up in our mailbox. Pretty typical for the first year after moving. Of course I quickly forwarded the misdirected bills, cards, and magazines. Lucky for me, a calendar arrived one day that introduced me to a new artist. It was just a typical advertising calendar for an insurance company, but with amazing, detailed paintings on each page created by Ken Zylla. I knew immediately that Zylla's images would be ideal for use with all ages, and I have used his work in dozens of lessons since. Zylla reminds me of Norman Rockwell in some ways: attention to detail, a fondness for Americana, and the ability to capture the sweetness of days gone by. He is well known for his nostalgic calendars.

Ken Zylla officially retired in 2011, but has left us with hundreds of images that are easy to view, easy to talk about, easy to make connections to. Browse Google Images for Ken's work and visit his website, www.kenzylla.com. His "America Remembered" calendar series is ideal for image reading.

To foster great thinking about Zylla's images, I model the Visible Thinking protocol, *SeeThinkWonder*, from Harvard University's Project Zero. The Visible Thinking protocol is simple yet powerful, and a way to easily structure image reading for students who are just getting started. It's a routine you can use to explore works of art . . . and really anything interesting! It makes the viewer slow down and think about what they see.

http://bit.ly/VXlYUj

So easy to use. And so valuable at the same time. I project one of Zylla's images that is chock full of details, like *Country Barn Dance*, *At the Movies*, *Junkyard Cops 'n' Robbers*, or *Reflections of Main Street*. The SeeThinkWonder Routine provides a purpose for students when viewing a common image. Just as I provide a purpose for reading a common text, I provide a purpose for the viewing of a common image.

In my book *Comprehension Connections* (Heinemann, 2007), each chapter contains a section called "Sensory Exercises" that highlights recommended art and artists, along with ideas for viewing and thinking. Or perhaps you have a favorite artist to share with your students, or a collection of images on hand to use. No matter. The important thing is to provide time to see and talk.

For a comprehensive list of questions to prompt deeper image reading see Jim Burke's classic, *Reading Reminders: Tools, Tips, and Techniques* (Boynton/Cook, 2000). Burke asks dozens of questions, from as simple as "Why are we looking at this?" to the complex "What do we need to know to read this image successfully?"

The world around us is exploding with visual images. Our students deserve time for instruction and practice in making meaning of this critical literacy.

Read to Learn More About the Genre

The following authors/series encourage us to slow down and get inside of an image. Each present images in a unique way, calling for sharp eyes, the ability to look from every angle and *see* the world differently. These books work well in a whole-group setting when the images are projected onto a screen, or with partners viewing the images up close and personal.

Anna Nilsen

www.annanilsen.com

- *Art Auction Mystery.* Boston: Kingfisher, 2005.
- *Art Fraud Detective.* Boston: Kingfisher, 2003.
- *The Great Art Scandal: Solve the Crime, Save the Show.* Boston: Kingfisher, 2000.

Bob Raczka

The "Bob Raczka's Art Adventures" Series
www.bobraczka.com

- *3-D ABC: A Sculptural Alphabet.* Minneapolis: First Avenue Editions, 2007.
- *Art Is . . . .* Minneapolis: Millbrook Press, 2003.
- *Here's Looking at Me: How Artists See Themselves.* Minneapolis: Millbrook Press, 2006.
- *More Than Meets the Eye: Seeing Art with All Five Senses.* Minneapolis: Millbrook Press, 2003.
- *Name That Style: All About Isms in Art.* Minneapolis: Millbrook Press, 2009.
- *No One Saw.* Minneapolis: Millbrook Press, 2001.
- *The Vermeer Interviews: Conversations with Seven Works of Art.* Minneapolis: First Avenue Editions, 2010.
- *Unlikely Pairs: Fun with Famous Works of Art.* Minneapolis: Millbrook Press, 2005.

Gillian Wolfe

The "LOOK" Series

- *LOOK! Body Language in Art.* London: Frances Lincoln, 2009.
- *LOOK! Drawing the Line in Art.* London: Frances Lincoln, 2008.
- *LOOK! Really Smart Art.* London: Frances Lincoln, 2010.
- *LOOK! Seeing the Light in Art.* London: Frances Lincoln, 2010.
- *LOOK! Zoom in on Art.* London: Frances Lincoln, 2007.

The Metropolitan Museum of Art

The "Can You Find It?" Series

- Cressy, Judith. 2002. *Can You Find It?: Search and Discover More Than 150 Details in 19 Works of Art.* New York: Abrams.
- Cressy, Judith. 2004. *Can You Find It, Too?: Search and Discover More Than 150 Details in 20 Works of Art.* 2004. New York: Abrams.
- Falken, Linda. 2010. *Can You Find It?: America.* New York: Abrams.
- Schulte, Jessica. 2005. *Can You Find It Inside?: Search and Discover for Young Art Lovers.* New York: Abrams.
- Schulte, Jessica. 2005. *Can You Find It Outside?: Search and Discover for Young Art Lovers.* New York: Abrams.

Quotations About Images to Get Kids Talking

Using quotations is a great way to dwell, if only for a moment, in the deep thought of another. These quotations help us think more deeply about the image: in books, in photography, and in the media.

> *"One rainy Sunday when I was in the third grade, I picked up a book to look at the pictures and discovered that even though I did not want to, I was reading. I have been a reader ever since."*
> **—Beverly Cleary**

"Pictures help you to form the mental mold."
—**Robert Collier**

"The source and center of all man's creative power . . .
is his power of making images, or the power of imagination."
—**Robert Collier**

"Whoever controls the media, the images, controls the culture."
—**Allen Ginsberg**

"A photograph is usually looked at—seldom looked into."
—**Ansel Adams**

"A camera can photograph thought."
—**Dirk Bogarde**

"What is the use of a book, thought Alice,
without pictures or conversations?"
—**Lewis Carroll**

"Words and pictures can work together to communicate
more powerfully than either alone."
—**William Albert Allard**

"The image is more than an idea. It is a vortex or cluster
of fused ideas and is endowed with energy."
—**Ezra Pound**

"The soul cannot think without a picture."
—**Aristotle**

Time for Text: More About Image Reading

Each of the books listed below has helped me bridge this launching sequence to thinking-intensive reading and writing lessons. From graphic novels to digital storytelling, you'll find a wide variety of options to further explore the genre.

- Booth, David. 2006. *Reading Doesn't Matter Anymore*. Markham, ON: Pembroke.

- Frey, Nancy, and Douglas Fisher. 2008. *Teaching Visual Literacy*. Thousand Oaks, CA: Corwin Press.

- Kajder, Sara. 2006. *Bringing the Outside In*. Portland, ME: Stenhouse.

- Kist, William. 2009. *The Socially Networked Classroom: Teaching in the New Media Age*. Thousand Oaks, CA: Corwin Press.

- Thurman, Mark, and Emily Hearn. 2010. *Get Graphic*. Markham, ON: Pembroke.

- Thompson, Terry. 2008. *Adventures in Graphica*. Portland, ME: Stenhouse.

- Walling, Donovan R. 2005. *Visual Knowing*. Thousand Oaks, CA: Corwin Press.

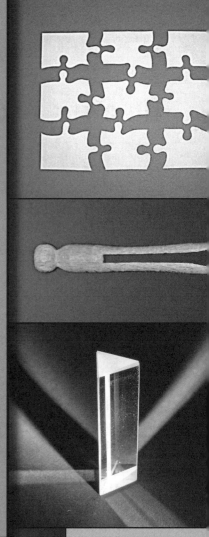

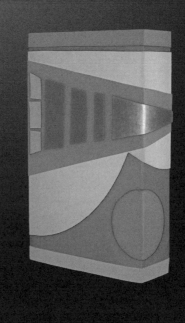

seeds

7

Biography, Autobiography, and Memoir

Such Is Life

"Is there anything you want to ask me?"

—Janet McGregor (1914–2007)

Janet loved stories. For as long as I knew her, not an afternoon passed without an episode of *Days of Our Lives* and a couple of hours with a paperback in hand. Whether at home, visiting family, or on the road, Janet had a book tucked into her purse, ready for any quiet moment that might arise. I never asked her the question, but I infer that her favorite genre to read was romantic fiction. Coming in at a close second, however, had to be the memoir. And not just any memoir. Her own memoirs. For the twelve years that I was lucky enough to experience the intersection between her life and mine, Janet was constantly writing and rereading her memoirs. To make sure she wasn't leaving anything out, Janet asked the same question dozens and dozens of times: "Is there anything you want to ask me?" Janet wanted, I believe, more than almost anything, to leave behind her story. The story of her happy childhood in the Allegheny Mountains, of the years teaching music in rural Pennsylvania, of falling in love with Robert McGregor, of raising a family in a college town in Ohio.

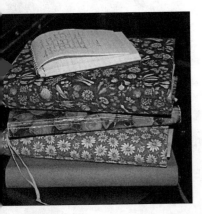

Fig. 7-1 Janet's notebooks

For quite a while, Janet was quietly writing her memoirs, filling notebooks with her distinctive cursive, mostly in ink, sometimes in pencil. She wrote about her past and about the people in her past. She chronicled her travels since retirement and left little to the imagination. The longer Janet lived, the more important it became to her to make her story public, to ensure the likelihood that it would endure long after she'd left us behind. I believe she wrote her story out of a longing—a longing that the history she'd lived and the people she'd loved would be forever remembered, but she also wrote it out of love—the kind of love that wants to keep on giving to others in an infinite way.

Janet taught me about this genre. Because of her persistence and dedication to the completion of her own memoirs, I began to understand the power and layered meaning in the writing and the reading of this kind of text. It's a genre of emotion and meaning, for both the writer and the reader. I learned so much about her, my mother-in-law, from the words she left behind, and in the meantime learned about myself. Author Heather Lattimer says, "Making sense of memoirs enables us to make sense of our lives" (2003). To me, that's the interesting thing about these similar genres: biography, autobiography, and memoir. The reader takes a peek into the life of someone else, and all the while sees her own life more clearly.

What's biography? The story of someone's life written or told by another person.

What's autobiography? The story of someone's life written or told by themselves.

What's memoir? It's like autobiography but not as formal or complete. A memoir might only be about a brief moment in time. Journals and diaries fall into the same subgenre, but are less story-like and often the entries are arranged chronologically.

Why should we read biography, autobiography, and memoir?

- To preserve memories and personal histories
- To encourage reflection
- To interpret stories in context
- To foster the understanding of others

Launching Sequence: Biography, Autobiography, and Memoir

Concrete Experience: Mirror, Mirror

Biography and autobiography. When I was in school, I could never remember which one was which. The names of these genres always seemed like they should be the other way around. Maybe it was just me. I do know, however, that the names of these genres aren't so commonly used that students know them right away. I'm sure it would have helped me to have dissected the names of these genres, to know that *auto-* means self, that *bio-* means life, and that *graph* means written. But a concrete experience would also have been a good way to guide me to a general understanding of each genre and to link a label to them . . . to notice and name. As Peter Johnston taught me in *Choice Words* (Stenhouse, 2004), once you start noticing and naming things (genres, in this case), it's hard to stop! Since I know my students need this concrete approach as well, I launch the genres of biography and autobiography with a fun, simple object lesson.

I start with a medium-sized, handheld mirror, the kind you likely have at home. Standing with my back to the class (I try not to do this too often!) and holding the mirror up, I slowly move it around so I can see all of my students' faces. I announce that I'm going to use this mirror to help them understand the major difference between two genres. If I've already launched other genres at this point in the year, and it is likely that I have, I'll refer to the "genre wall" where the names of previously explored genres are posted. Kids will know they're in store for something new.

I tell my students that I'm looking for a particular student in the class. Attentiveness is never in short supply at this moment! I stop moving the mirror when I find a student who won't mind being in the spotlight for a while. While looking at this student in the mirror, still with my back to the class, I begin to tell what I know of his/her life story.

"I see Tony. He was born right here in Ohio and has lived here his whole life. He has an older sister, Mari, who is in high school now. Tony loves the Cincinnati Bengals and wants to be a professional football player someday."

Then I pause for a moment to turn and face the class, asking them to turn and talk to each other, noticing what just happened. "What did I do? What did I say? How could this be like a genre that we'll soon learn about?" I cruise around and listen in to their responses, withholding comment, then call everyone back to attention.

"Now watch and listen as I change what I'm doing and saying."

This time I face the class, still holding my mirror up but this time looking into it at myself. (At this point I am momentarily distracted by how much I'm beginning to look like my mother.)

"I see myself. I was born in Arizona but have made Ohio my home. I have a sister named Holly who is four years younger than I am. I love traveling and want to return to Brazil one of these days."

I move the mirror aside and allow for some processing time before I prompt the turn and talk.

"Now turn and talk once more. What did I do this time? What did I say? How was it different from the first example when I was focused on Tony? Can you think of any genres that these concrete experiences might represent?"

If my students have a lot of schema about genres, I provide less guidance and allow them to construct more from the experience. However, if this might be their first exposure to these genres, I'll guide them along as necessary to understanding.

Below are a few student responses from my experiences with various grade levels:

"The first time you talked about someone else.
The second time you talked about yourself."
—Julian

"You stayed on the topic both times."
—Maggie

"A genre might always be about someone's life and describe it."
—Kenyon

"I have read stories where it is all about someone famous
and it tells when they were born and when they died
and about all of the things they did."
—Casey

"When I was in second grade I wrote a story about my life."
—Paige

Each student response usually generates more thinking from other students until we start getting closer to what the genres of biography and autobiography are all about. When I'm satisfied that the students have a basic understanding, we add the names of these genres to the genre chart.

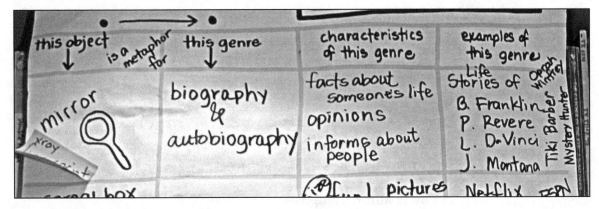

Fig. 7.2 A snippet from the ongoing genre chart

Noticing and Naming the Genre on Their Own

These genres are easy to find. If you can, take students to a school or local library to see what kinds of books line the biography shelves. Or take a few snapshots in the biography section of a local library or bookstore to share with your class. They'll love to see a few titles from your personal library, too.

Make students aware of the role these genres play in popular culture. The sales of biography, autobiography, and memoir have been increasing since the 1990s. In fact, in 2007, publishers acquired more memoirs than novels by first-time authors.

To give students experience with these genres, I gather a dozen or so picture books and place them in a shopping bag. The bag is filled with biographies and autobiographies, including a few that will look familiar to my students and some new titles as well. In a large group, I build suspense by telling the class that I'll reveal the books one at a time, provide a bit of evidence, allow for a turn and talk, then place the books on display for independent reading selections.

As I raise a title from the bag, I ask the students to listen to the few clues I provide, then turn and whisper to a friend, and identify each as biography or auto-biography. A few have the word "memoir" in the title, giving students a chance to think about the subtleties of the semantics. Kids always love the chance to hear about new books and talk to a friend in this comfortable context. Gather your own collection or get ideas from this list of my favorites:

Picture book biographies

■ Biographies by Doreen Rappaport, which include *Abe's Honest Words*, *Jack's Path of Courage*, *John's Secret Dreams*, *Eleanor: Quiet No More*, and *Martin's Big Words*

■ DK Biography Series, which includes *Pele'*, *Gandhi*, *Amelia Earhart*, *Barack Obama*, and *Albert Einstein*

■ Graphic Biographies Series, which includes *Mother Jones*, *Jim Thorpe*, *Florence Nightingale*, and *Samuel Adams*

Picture book autobiographies

■ *Bill Peet: An Autobiography* by Bill Peet

■ *A Bookworm Who Hatched* by Verna Aardema

■ *26 Fairmount Avenue* by Tomie DePaola

■ *The Abracadabra Kid: A Writer's Life* by Sid Fleischman

■ *Boy: Tales of Childhood* by Roald Dahl

■ *West from Home: Letters of Laura Ingalls Wilder* by Laura Ingalls Wilder

■ *A Girl from Yamhill: A Memoir* by Beverly Cleary

And, of course, kids can explore on their own, by visiting amazing biography websites like these:

■ http://www.biography.com/bio4kids/index.jsp

■ http://incredible-people.com/

■ http://www.bbc.co.uk/history/historic_figures/

■ http://gardenofpraise.com/leaders.htm

Sensory Exercises:
Biography, Autobiography, Memoir
Music Connection: Lyrics About a Life

It's not uncommon for songwriters and musicians to use their talents to tell their own stories and the stories of others. So, making biography, autobiography, and memoir interesting and engaging for students is easily accomplished through music. With these genres, I've had great success with listening first, talking next, and reading last. But of course there are many paths you can take to guide your students to an understanding of these genres. And with lyrics and recorded music now at our fingertips for little or no cost, the ease of composing a music-supported lesson is a beautiful thing.

Biographical and autobiographical lyrics are present in many musical genres. They're probably present in your own music library. I tell my students that we can read a life, view a life, or in this case, hear a life. Here are a few of my favorite tunes with biographical or autobiographical lyrics. Be on the lookout for ways to connect the lyrics with social studies and science content.

Songs/albums with biographical lyrics (the singer sings about the life of another person):

- *Sister Rosa Parks* by the Neville Brothers. This song tells of courageous Rosa and how she changed the world in Montgomery, Alabama in 1955.

- *Sing in Portuguese* by Randy Stonehill. A touching song that chronicles the life and death of Randy's grandmother.

- *26 Scientists, Volume 1* and *26 Scientists, Volume 2* by Artichoke. These albums contain songs about scientists who made significant contributions to the world. Check for appropriate language prior to use in the classroom.

- *Man of Colours* by Icehouse. The lyrics tell of American painter, Andrew Wyeth.

- *Jacques Cousteau* by Livingston Taylor. A humorous but factual look at the life of French marine researcher, Jacques Cousteau.

Songs with autobiographical lyrics/memoir (the singer sings about his/her own life):

- "Childhood" by Michael Jackson. Honest, emotional lyrics from the King of Pop.

- "My Father" by Judy Collins. Although the song's title suggests biographical content, the lyrics are more autobiographical, allowing a glimpse into Judy's life.

- "Coal Miner's Daughter" by Loretta Lynn. The lyrics make it easy to visualize Loretta's early life in Butcher Holler (Hollow), Kentucky.

- "Way Back Home" by Phil Keaggy. Phil describes his childhood home and wonders what happens when people don't stop to remember their youth.

- "That Was Me" by Paul McCartney. Paul's life in a nutshell; background knowledge about the Beatles a plus.

Fig. 7.3 Listening with lyrics in hand

You might take a look in *Comprehension Connections* (Heinemann, 2007) for other song suggestions that belong in this genre, like Janis Ian's *At Seventeen* or Dolly Parton's *Coat of Many Colors.*

These "genre songs" can be used in a variety of ways. Try listening to a song in its entirety first, then identify the genre afterward. Have students partner up with some lyrics to read together. What makes these lyrics biographical? Autobiographical? Do the lyrics describe more of a moment than a lifetime? Might you classify them as memoir? Listen to the song again with lyrics on hand, and discuss with a partner, with table groups, or the whole class. View photographs of the person featured while thinking about his/her life.

Use the web to help you find just the song lyrics you're looking for. Lyric "warehouses" abound, but here are a few to try:

www.lyrics.com/

music.yahoo.com/lyrics

www.lyricscafe.com/lyricscafe/index.php

www.sing365.com/index.html

www.lyricsfreak.com/

www.songlyrics.com/az-lyrics/

www.azlyrics.com/a.html

www.lyricsmania.com/

Art Connection: Every Painter Paints Himself

Pair art and artists with the genres of biography, autobiography, and memoir for the perfect instructional match. The Tuscan proverb, "Ogni pittore dipinge sè," translates to "every painter paints himself." This idea has sometimes been taken literally, in that some painters have tended to make figures that look strangely like themselves, but most often is interpreted that the artist creates from his own view of the world and creates a reality true to self.

It's not difficult to find examples of biographical works (the artist portrays another person), and autobiographical works (the artist portrays himself). Here are a few well-known paintings, drawings, and photographs that mirror the focus genres of this chapter.

Portraits: Visual Biographies

- Leonardo da Vinci, *Mona Lisa*, 1503–1519
- Johannes (Jan) Vermeer, *Girl with a Pearl Earring*, circa 1665
- Thomas Sully, *Lady with a Harp: Eliza Ridgely*, 1818
- John Singer Sargent, *Theodore Roosevelt*, 1903
- Henri Matisse, *Portrait of Madame Matisse*, 1905
- Andy Warhol, *Marilyn Diptych*, 1962
- Alice Neel, *Faith Ringgold*, 1977
- David Hockney, *Mum*, 1988–1989

Self-Portraits: Visual Autobiographies

- Albrecht Dürer, *Self-portrait*, 1493
- Rembrandt Harmenszoon van Rijn, *Self-portrait*, 1660
- Mary Cassatt, *Portrait of the Artist*, 1878
- Pablo Picasso, *Self-portrait*, 1899–1900
- Camille Pissarro, *Self-portrait*, 1903
- Frida Kahlo, *Self-portrait*, 1940
- Cindy Sherman, *Untitled A*, 1975
- Chuck Close, *Self-portrait*, 1997

Apply the "See, Think, Wonder" routine to a few of these portraits. Play detective and look for "telling" clues. Draw inferences and cite evidence. Explore similarities and differences in biographies, autobiographies, and memoirs when interpreted through text versus music versus image. Dwelling with these images, spending time noticing details, can bring your students to a deeper understanding of the genres and make them better at image reading at the same time.

After launching these genres with a concrete experience and exploring the genres through music and art, your students are likely to have something to say. Making space for their thoughts and opinions is always important, even when new learning is emerging. Pose a few of these questions to see what your students are thinking.

- Would you rather read biography or autobiography? What makes you say that?

- Would you rather write about your own story or the story of someone else? Why?

- If you could learn about and write the life story of anyone who has ever lived, who would it be? Why is this person so interesting to you?

- How can music and art be autobiographical?

- Do you think you will ever want to write your memoirs? Why do you think it is important to so many people to have written their memoirs before they die?

- Do you think it is important for 100 percent of a biography or autobiography to be accurate? Explain your thinking.

- If a biography, autobiography, or memoir contains untruths or half-truths, should it be classified as another type of genre? Elaborate on your thinking.

Read to Learn More About the Genre

Read a biography written by Doreen Rappaport, and you'll soon discover a history-changing life story. Rappaport teams with amazingly talented illustrators and peppers the text with quotations. Author and illustrator's notes finish out each volume, along with timelines of important events. Her books are a joy to share with students of all ages.

Abe's Honest Words. New York: Hyperion, 2008.

Eleanor, Quiet No More. New York: Hyperion, 2009.

Jack's Path of Courage: The Life of John F. Kennedy. New York: Hyperion, 2010.

John's Secret Dreams. New York: Hyperion, 2004.

Lady Liberty: A Biography. Somerville, MA: Candlewick Press, 2008.

Martin's Big Words. New York: Hyperion, 2001.

Quotations About Biography, Autobiography, and Memoir to Get Kids Talking

Not only do people delight in writing their own life stories and the stories of others, they also enjoy talking about the genres—what they believe about "lifewriting" and why life stories are so important. Quotations on these topics abound. The following collection will spur new thinking for you and your students as you talk together.

*"Once you begin to write the true story of your life
in a form that anyone would possibly want to read,
you start to make compromises with the truth."*
—Ben Yagoda

*"A memoir is how one remembers one's own life,
while an autobiography is history, requiring research,
date, facts double-checked."*
—Gore Vidal

*"We should probably all pause to confront our past from time to
time, because it changes its meaning as our circumstances alter."*
—Karen Armstrong

*"An autobiography is an obituary in serial form
with the last installment missing."*
—Quentin Crisp

*"I believe that the memoir is the novel of the 21st century;
it's an amazing form that we haven't even begun to tap . . .
we're just getting started figuring out what the rules are."*
—Susan Cheever

*"Actually, the true story of a person's life can never be written. It
is beyond the power of literature. The full tale of any life would be
both utterly boring and utterly unbelievable."*
—Isaac Bashevis

*"Memoir is how we try to make sense of who we are,
who we once were, and what values and heritage shaped us."*
—William Zinsser

*"An autobiography usually reveals nothing bad about its writer
except his memory."*
—Franklin P. Jones

*"Everybody needs his memories.
They keep the wolf of insignificance from the door."*
—Saul Bellow

*"Autobiography may be the preeminent kind
of American expression."*
—Henry James

*"Biographies are but the clothes and buttons of the man.
The biography of the man himself cannot be written."*
—Mark Twain

"An autobiography is the story of how a man thinks he lived."
—Herbert Samuel

*"For one who reads, there is no limit to the number
of lives that may be lived, for fiction, biography,
and history offer an inexhaustible number of lives
in many parts of the world, in all periods of time."*
—Louis L'Amour

*"Perfect objectivity is always impossible,
no matter who writes a person's biography."*
—Pamela Stephenson

*"An autobiography is a book a person writes about his own life
and it is usually full of all sorts of boring details."*
—Roald Dahl

Time for Text: More About Teaching Biography, Autobiography, and Memoir

Now that you've taken your students from the concrete to the abstract, it's time to go deeper with these genres. This short but powerful list of resources will get you started.

- Bomer, Katherine. 2005. *Writing a Life: Teaching Memoir to Sharpen Insight, Shape Meaning—and Triumph Over Tests*. Portsmouth, NH: Heinemann.

- Fletcher, Ralph. 2011. *Mentor Author, Mentor Texts: Short Texts, Craft Notes, and Practical Classroom Uses*. Portsmouth, NH: Heinemann.

- Lattimer, Heather. 2003. *Thinking Through Genre: Units of Study in Reading and Writing Workshops Grades 4–12*. Portland, ME: Stenhouse.

- Zarnowski, Myra. 2003. *A Questioning Approach to Reading and Writing Biographies*. Portsmouth, NH: Heinemann.

seeds

8

Informational Text

The Need to Know

"Information is the oxygen of the modern age. It seeps through the walls topped by barbed wire, it wafts across the electrified borders."

—Ronald Reagan

ere's what I've observed about informational text: It is everywhere . . . and it's important to everyone, every day. My dad was my first example of this. Every Saturday and Sunday, every weekend of my childhood, Dad put his to-do list aside to read the newspaper. Weekend subscriptions weren't available, so Dad would get up early, hop in the car, and come home a few minutes later with a copy of the *Cincinnati Enquirer* and a fruit-filled doughnut from Bonnie Lynn Bakery. (Now that I think about it, maybe the pastry was the true motivator!) There was yard work to do, and there were church events to attend, but Dad made time to get that daily dose of information he craved. Weather. Sports. Politics. The local news. Now Dad is retired and gets to read the paper every morning. When I visit, the first thing I see when I stroll to the kitchen for breakfast is Dad sitting at the table with the *Naples Daily News*, a cup of coffee, and yes, sometimes even a doughnut. What else have I noticed Dad reading? How-to manuals, brochures, Internet articles . . . anything where there's information to be learned in a quick, succinct manner. The funny thing is that my dad doesn't consider himself to be a reader. Like many people, he thinks one must enjoy reading thick novels to belong to the "reading club." But Dad's affinity for information, and the time he has devoted to the reading of it in his seventy plus years, grants him membership into the club . . . with distinction.

When I look back over my life, informational text is the genre I've relied upon to help me through important (and sometimes trying) times. When I got a Border collie puppy. When I traveled to Brazil without my family. When my mom was diagnosed with macular degeneration. When I needed to learn how to pitch a manuscript idea to a publisher. Informational text has, at times, comforted me, alarmed me, satisfied and educated me. It's ironic: for such an objective, no-room-for-error kind of genre, informational text can still be so personal.

Another thing I've noticed about this genre is that it nudges me into the realm of doing. Sometimes, of course, I read, I'm informed, and that's that. But many more times, I read, I'm informed, and I take action. I read about a possible drug interaction? I call my pharmacist. I read about an upcoming Lyle Lovett concert? I buy tickets. I read about a local foundation that is supporting families of children with cancer? I make a donation. We can call this "generative knowledge." As David Perkins says, "Knowledge does not just sit there but functions richly in people's lives to help them understand and deal with the world."

Scholar Theodore Roszak puts it like this:

> The original root of the word information is the Latin word *in-formare*, which means to fashion, shape, or create, to give form to. Information is an idea that has been given a form, such as the spoken or written word. It is a means of representing an image or thought so that it can be communicated from one mind to another. Rather than worrying about all the information afloat in the world, we must ask ourselves what matters to us, what do we want to know. It's having ideas and learning to deal with issues that is important, not accumulating lots and lots of data.

When launching this genre, we need to remember that *reading* informational text is sometimes just the first step. As with any genre, it's our thinking that makes the information come alive. In *Comprehension & Collaboration* (Heinemann, 2009), Stephanie Harvey and Harvey Daniels remind us that "[c]omprehension begins to take root only when we merge our thinking with the information."

So how does this trickle down into the classroom? Well, let's teach kids what informational text is. *It's a subset of nonfiction. Its primary purpose is to inform. It uses specialized language and conventions. It encompasses topics that appeal to everyone.* But let's not stop there. Let's teach kids about what informational text can do . . . or prompt us to do. Let's teach them to blend their thinking with the information they read to maximize the chances that it will make a positive difference in our world.

Launching Sequence:
Informational Text

Concrete Experience: Seed Packets

By now you know that the concrete items I suggest in my launching lessons are accessible and inexpensive. This time is no exception. A great little place to find informational text, with accompanying images, maps, and graphics, is a good old-fashioned seed packet. Buy some at the hardware store or local discount department store. For right around $1.00 per packet, you'll have an example of informational text that kids can hold in their hands.

I begin by letting my students know that we'll be exploring a new genre together. I might choose to name the genre right then and there, or to allow for conversation and conjecture throughout my think-aloud. It all depends on the time I have and the level of their familiarity with this genre.

I show my students a packet of seeds, and tell them that I'm holding an amazing thing in my hands, proof that good things often come in small packages. After giving them a chance to turn and talk to each other about the concrete object I'm using to launch this lesson, and if/when they've seen a seed packet before, I ask the students to listen in as I think aloud. Their job is to listen closely to my thinking as I process informational text. If I'm working with intermediate students, I might have them jot down what they notice while I think aloud. If possible, I use a document camera to project the front and back of the packet as I refer to it. I want the kids to see what I'm talking about. If a document camera is not available, I might make a copy of the packet for partners to share, or project photographs of both sides of the packet.

"Wow. There's so much information here. It's only a 3" × 4½" packet, but there's text, images, and a map with a map key. I can learn a lot from spending a few minutes reading and thinking about what I see."

I begin with the front of the packet, commenting about the class (Garden bean) and the variety name (Bushmaster).

"I'm noticing the color picture. Gosh, these beans look just like the green beans my grandma grew in her garden in Kentucky. I already knew this plant belongs to the vegetable category. But if I hadn't known that, the company labeled the packet as such right at the top of the packet. And that's not all I see on the front. There are some quick facts in the bottom right-hand corner. Not much text there, but since they put it on the front it is probably very important. These garden beans need full sun and it takes seventy days for the beans to be fully grown. It's interesting how this seed company uses symbols along with the text to help me understand: a sun to show the amount of light the beans need, a basket to show how long it takes until harvest, and a flowerpot to show that the bean can be grown in a container. Hmmm. I never thought about growing green beans in a pot or flower box. That's cool! I wonder if many people do that."

I continue my think-aloud while reading the information on the back of the packet.

"There seems to be a short summary about this plant at the top. 'Long-lasting plants produce a high yield of stringless, green pods.' Must not be the same variety that my grandma grew. Those always had strings. I wonder how many different varieties of green beans there are. This summary is important, so they used bold type and placed it at the top and in the center."

To support the students, and to give them a chance to talk about what they're noticing, I take a break from my think-aloud so they can turn and talk. After a minute or two, I finish thinking aloud.

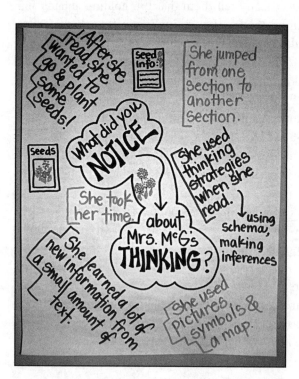

Fig. 8-1 A record of what students noticed during the think-aloud

"Here are a few little pictures that illustrate how deep to plant each seed and how far apart it should be from other seeds. All of that information is on the left side. On the right side, the text is written in sentence form, providing me with detailed sowing instructions. There's a QR code in the middle that I could scan with my phone if I need even more info from the company's website. I'm guessing that is a relatively new feature, added in the past few years. And last but not least, here's a color-coded U.S. map that lets me know the best months for planting in my area of the country. It's amazing . . . I know so much more than I did just minutes ago. Having all of this information makes me want to go home and plant these seeds!"

Again, I encourage the kids to talk to each other, sharing what they noticed about my thinking as I read the information. The level of their own thinking about text shapes their responses, of course. How much experience they have noticing the thinking of others also comes into play.

Noticing and Naming the Genre on Their Own

Let's extend the concrete experience and allow students time to make some discoveries. Provide seed packets for partners. Use vegetable, flowers, herbs, and fruit. Using packets from the same company makes it easier to compare similar features and have conversation across groups later. And, of course, kids want to hold the seeds.

Fig. 8-2 Morning glory seeds

Encourage students to view, talk, and notice. In essence, I want kids to begin doing their own think-alouds as I walk around listening in. This time, though, the tables have turned. It's me jotting down notes about their thinking. I share some highlights with them after partner time is finished.

"Janie read some new information about morning glories and shared it with Jacob. They didn't know that these flowers can grow up to six feet! Jacob had heard that morning glories are poisonous, but they couldn't find supporting evidence for that in the text. Time for some research, right Jacob?

"Curtis and Livvy did an amazing job with the informational text on their lupine seed packet. As I listened in, it sounded like detective work. Curtis questioned why the company used so many pictures on the front and so much text on the back. Livvy interpreted the map and found that lupines would not likely do well here because of our hot summers."

After I share a few observations, each pair of students joins up with another pair. These small groups notice and name the genre together for a few minutes, then we pause to consider the name for the genre represented on the seed packets.

"Informational text is one way to categorize this genre. What other genre labels might work? After viewing, reading, and talking, what are you thinking now?"

Linden suggests "nonfiction," Reggie says "it's like a Wiki page," and Myra notices that "it's facts, not story." James asks, "Can we have these seeds? We should plant them before summer starts!"

And that's about it for launching, noticing, and naming. I refrain from teaching lengthy minilessons about informational text, from assigning the classic worksheet that matches features with the genres. Instead, we use something concrete and relevant, we experience the text with conversation in a nonevaluative way, and notice how it compares with other kinds of texts we've read. Students are engaged and motivated. And as far as I know, that's the best way to begin.

Note: Your students might be interested to see how a seed company teaches customers how to understand the informational text on their products. Visit www.burpee.com, click on "how-to videos," then find the video titled "How to Read a Seed Packet."

Sensory Exercises:
Informational Text

Music Connection: Schoolhouse Rock

It hurts, but it's true: before some of you were born, I was in high school. And when my sophomore English teacher took an extended leave of absence, a substitute teacher was hired. Not just any substitute teacher, but a *cool* one. She used song lyrics for our text and played the music while we read. I remember being engaged by the text during class, and looked forward to what the next day would hold.

Lyrics are underutilized in our classrooms. We have thousands of crafted, meaningful sets of lyrics at our fingertips, lyrics that cross generations and genres. Lyrics are super-powered, with several advantages when it comes to text choice: brevity, meaning, and music. Often the text fits on one page. The songwriter crafts the text so that the words are saturated with meaning. The music supports the reader, stirring emotion and prompting the brain to make connections to prior knowledge. When it comes to text selection, song lyrics are the perfect storm.

Why not use the advantages offered by song lyrics when learning to read informational text? Your personal music collection is a good place to start. You might already own recordings that are informational in genre. If not, there are many places that house song lyrics for easy access. A well-stocked educational song website to explore is www.songsforteaching.com. Here you'll find thousands of songs with informational lyrics, searchable by content area and subject. Some songs are for purchase; others have printable lyrics available at little or no cost. Find songs about the water cycle, linear equations, American history, and more.

The quintessential model for informational text in lyric form is found in the songs of *Schoolhouse Rock!* Just because *SHR* has been around since the 1970s doesn't weaken its usefulness and appeal. The vintage *SHR* songs inform and entertain just as much as ever. And even though the first animated songs were aired in 1973, new episodes were released as recently as 2009. Perhaps you have not been exposed to *Schoolhouse Rock!*, or maybe it has been a while since you thought about it. The background behind *Schoolhouse Rock!* is quite interesting. Creator David McCall noticed how one of his sons knew the lyrics to rock songs, but had difficulty recalling academic information. So McCall worked in collaboration with colleagues to release songs to help kids learn and remember important information, and before long, accompanying animation was added. Through the decades, millions of kids (and adults!) have met new information through *Schoolhouse Rock!* songs. Topics include science, history, math, grammar, and economics. Visit www.schoolhouse rock.tv to print some lyrics and experience informational text with your students through these topical tunes. On many of the lyric pages you'll find links to the YouTube videos. These videos and accompanying soundtracks are available for purchase at www.iTunes.com.

Art Connection: David McCandless

Have you ever felt bogged down by too much information, too fast? Have you seen this happen to your students? Might it be possible to start with informational text, and then take away most of the words, replacing them with beautiful colors and patterns? It is possible, and David McCandless has done it. McCandless takes complex, abstract information and makes it inviting, meaningful, and beautiful. A master of space and design, he can turn dry, lifeless data into a fascinating work of art. In fact, maybe that's a good way to describe David McCandless: an information artist.

"By visualizing information, we turn it into a landscape that you can explore with your eyes, a sort of information map. And when you're lost in information, an information map is kind of useful."

—David McCandless

Interpreting information through visual representation is crucial. The graphic depiction of information is all around our students: in texts, on tests, in their lives.

In *The Visual Miscellaneum* (2009), McCandless provides countless informational images that represent research findings. (Note: Since a wide range of topics is represented, not every page is suitable for elementary students. Some are appropriate, however, and are listed below.) A few months back, Harvey (Smokey) Daniels and I were exploring the power of the think-aloud with the K–12 teaching staff in the Federal Hocking School District in Southeastern Ohio. Of course we used more traditional informational text as part of our demonstration, but we modeled with a couple of pieces of visual information, as well. One graph clearly showed the percentages of children living in poverty from six countries. Another picture compared the amount of money that people promised in tsunami aid to the amount that was actually paid. Yet another infographic illustrated the annual amount of methane emissions from humans and animals. Yuck!

Here are a few of David McCandless's visual representations of information to prompt thinking and discussion in the classroom:

- Which Fish Are Okay to Eat? (research from the Marine Conservation Society)
- 30 Years Makes a Difference (the depletion of the Amazon rainforest)
- Types of Coffee (all kinds of combinations plus caffeine content)
- Water Towers (how much water it takes to accomplish daily tasks)
- Life Times (how we spend our lives)

Resources for teaching with infographics at the secondary level are easy to find. But reaching our younger learners with what McCandless calls "the language of the eye" is just as important. Listen to McCandless's classic TED talk at www.ted .com, visit his website at www.informationisbeautiful.net, and learn how to make information interesting and attractive. For ideas specific to classroom instruction, visit *The Learning Network*, a *New York Times* blog: http://learning.blogs.nytimes .com/ and read the post, "Teaching with Infographics/Places to Start" from August 23, 2010. This post is filled with links to content-specific information that is portrayed in visual ways.

Near the beginning of this chapter, I mentioned how often understanding information spurs me into action. McCandless speaks about this, too. He believes that if we can enhance the way we understand information, we can change our perspectives, and ultimately, change our behavior.

Read to Learn More About the Genre:
Orbis Pictus Award Winners

So we've launched the genre in a concrete way and looked through the lens of music and art. What's next? Some quality informational picture books would be great, but where can we find the best of the best? Look no further than the Orbis Pictus Awards . . . and my friend Fran Wilson.

Talk with Fran for even a few minutes and you'll know her family comes first; she's really proud of her husband and three children. Talk a little while longer and you'll hear all about her second-grade class at Madeira Elementary in Cincinnati, and about her undergraduate students at the University of Cincinnati. But Fran has an area of expertise from which we can all learn: informational text. Fran is the current chairperson for the Orbis Pictus Award for Outstanding Nonfiction for Children's Literature Committee. I spent a couple of hours with Fran today at a local coffee shop, and children's nonfiction was the topic du jour. Let me tell you a bit about Orbis Pictus, and then I'll share some words of wisdom from Fran.

Fig. 8-3 Tanny learns more about informational text from Fran Wilson

Back in 1990, the National Council of Teachers of English (NCTE) decided to honor children's nonfiction, as well as the authors and illustrators who create it. Children's fiction had long been appreciated, and the same distinction for nonfiction was overdue. Not only did NCTE desire to honor children's nonfiction, it wanted to support and encourage its use in the classroom. The Orbis Pictus Award was born. The award is named after the first children's picture book, *Orbis Pictus* (The World in Pictures), written by Johannes Amos Comenius, published in 1657.

A committee of seven, representing diversity in geographical location and in the educational roles of the committee members, reads and reviews hundreds of children's informational texts each year. Although only one book is chosen as the annual award winner, up to five additional books receive an honors designation, and eight others are listed as recommended titles. The awards are announced each January at www.ncte.org/awards/orbispictus.

The Orbis Pictus Committee follows a stringent selection process, valuing the following criteria:

- Accuracy
- Organization
- Design
- Style

Fran tells me that the relevance of each title and how it could enhance learning in the classroom is also considered. And that's where Fran's expertise comes in. She's a master of using nonfiction in her second-grade classroom. She uses books that are current and accurate, with ample evidence of a strong research base. Not only does she know how to *choose* informational text, she knows how to *use* it. Listen in on what Fran had to say at the coffee shop today.

On the importance of informational text in the twenty-first century:

> Kids have a natural desire to learn, and they're hungry for knowledge. Yet sometimes we gravitate toward fiction when an informational text is what is needed. There's nothing quite like having quality nonfiction in the classroom, seeing kids pore over the text with a partner or in a small group. They soak the text right in, set their own purpose, and get inspired to do research.

On the changes she's seen in this genre over the past decade:

> The visual appeal of children's nonfiction is so carefully done now: the layouts, the fonts with different purposes, the sidebars, photographs and illustrations. High quality, all of it. The text is important, but the overall design makes kids want to get it into their hands. The collage artwork in this year's Orbis Pictus Award winner, *Balloons Over Broadway*, is a good example. The other really big change I've noticed is the style of writing. Often it's like the author is in conversation with the children. It's not just fact, fact, fact. The details build suspense in an engaging way. Quality children's nonfiction is so engaging it competes with technology. There are still some formal nonfiction children's books; we continue to see some of those. But there are many with a new voice, a new perspective . . . books where kids can visualize the information because of the way it is written and presented.

On helping kids understand informational text:

> Let the text be the expert. We can't go in thinking we know it all.
> Read and acknowledge what the children see. Most of the time
> when I find a book I want to share, the kids will notice things
> that I didn't. Like this year when I used *Balloons Over Broad-
> way*, a student said, "This was a really important book because
> it showed problem solving." I had never looked at the text that
> way. Kids can identify important themes in the text and details
> in the illustrations that adults often miss. Give children a chance
> to think and talk about the information. This will support their
> understanding.

Fran's Do's and One Don't:

- DO share informational text frequently.

- DO establish a daily read-aloud for nonfiction.

- DO create a climate where kids feel free to discuss nonfiction, not just
  the contents of the text but how it was organized and put together.

- DO pay attention to content *and* craft. Ask, "What would the author
  have to do to write this book?" and "What choices did the author have
  to make when creating this book?"

- DO invite kids to think metacognitively about the craft and invite them
  to use what they notice in their own writing.

- DO include books that connect to the interests of your kids, and, on
  the flipside, introduce them to new topics with quality nonfiction. Make
  it a balance.

- DON'T read informational text aloud and quiz children on the contents.
  That can kill a great book. If kids start to look at nonfiction like a test,
  they won't want to read it.

Take advantage of the hard work and expertise that Fran Wilson and the
Orbis Pictus Committee have done on behalf of this genre. Look for these
high-quality informational picture books to enhance instruction across the day
in your classroom.

2012 Orbis Pictus Award Winner and Honor Books

- *Balloons over Broadway: The True Story of the Puppeteer of Macy's Parade* by Melissa Sweet (Houghton Mifflin Books for Children)
- *Amelia Lost: The Life and Disappearance of Amelia Earhart* by Candace Fleming (Schwartz & Wade Books)
- *Father Abraham: Lincoln and His Sons* by Harold Holzer (Calkins Creek)
- *Pablo Neruda: Poet of the People* by Monica Brown, illustrated by Julie Paschkis (Henry Holt & Company)
- *Terezin: Voices from the Holocaust* by Ruth Thomson (Candlewick Press)
- *The Mangrove Tree: Planting Trees to Feed Families* by Susan L. Roth and Cindy Trumbore (Lee & Low Books, Inc.)

2011 Orbis Pictus Award Winner and Honor Books

- *Ballet for Martha: Making Appalachian Spring* by Jan Greenberg and Sandra Jordan, illustrated by Brian Floca (Roaring Brook Press)
- *Birmingham Sunday* by Larry Dane Brimner (Calkins Creek)
- *Candy Bomber: The Story of the Berlin Airlift's "Chocolate Pilot"* by Michael O. Tunnell (Charlesbridge)
- *If Stones Could Speak: Unlocking the Secrets of Stonehenge* by Mark Aronson (National Geographic)
- *Journey into the Deep: Discovering New Ocean Creatures* by Rebecca L. Johnson (Millbrook Press)
- *Mammoths and Mastodons: Titans of the Ice Age* by Cheryl Bardoe (Abrams Books for Young Readers)

2010 Orbis Pictus Award Winner and Honor Books

- *The Secret World of Walter Anderson* by Hester Bass, illustrated by E. B. Lewis (Candlewick Press)
- *Almost Astronauts: 13 Women Who Dared to Dream* by Tanya Lee Stone (Candlewick Press)
- *Darwin: With Glimpses into His Private Journal and Letters* by Alice B. McGinty (Houghton Mifflin Books for Children)

- *The Frog Scientist* by Pamela S. Turner (Houghton Mifflin Books for Children)

- *How Many Baby Pandas?* by Sandra Markle (Walker Books for Young Readers)

- *Noah Webster: Weaver of Words* by Pegi Deitz Shea (Calkins Creek Books)

Quotations About Informational Text to Get Kids Talking

Not all of these quotations are specifically about informational *text*. Some help us think solely about information itself—how we use it and how it affects us.

"It is a very sad thing that nowadays there is so little useless information."
—Oscar Wilde

"Everybody gets so much information all day long that they lose their common sense."
—Gertrude Stein

"I find that a great part of the information I have was acquired by looking up something and finding something else on the way."
—Franklin P. Adams

"I was brought up to believe that the only thing worth doing was to add to the sum of accurate information in the world."
—Margaret Mead

"In your thirst for knowledge, be sure not to drown in all the information."
—Anthony J. D'Angelo

"Information's pretty thin stuff unless mixed with experience."
—Clarence Day

*"But with nonfiction, the task is very straightforward:
Do the research, tell the story."*
—**Laura Hillenbrand**

*"In nonfiction, you have that limitation,
that constraint, of telling the truth."*
—**Peter Matthiessen**

"Facts are to the mind what food is to the body."
—**Edmund Burke**

"Seek truth from facts."
—**Deng Xiaoping**

Time for Text: Informational Text

Take it to the next level with the lesson ideas in the following resources. Mix these instructional approaches with informational text that appeals to the interests of your students. Both student engagement and learning will soar!

- Duke, Nell, and V. Susan Bennett-Armistead. 2003. *Reading and Writing Informational Text in the Primary Grades*. New York: Scholastic.

- Gear, Adrienne. 2008. *Nonfiction Reading Power: Teaching Students to Think While They Read All Kinds of Information*. Markham, ON: Pembroke.

- Harvey, Stephanie, and Anne Goudvis. 2008. *The Comprehension Toolkit: Language and Lessons for Active Literacy, Grades 3–6*. Portsmouth, NH: Heinemann.

- Harvey, Stephanie, and Anne Goudvis. 2008. *The Primary Comprehension Toolkit: Language and Lessons for Active Literacy, Grades K–2*. Portsmouth, NH: Heinemann.

- Hoyt, Linda. 2002. *Make It Real*. Portsmouth, NH: Heinemann.

- Hoyt, Linda. 2003. *Navigating Informational Texts: Easy and Explicit Strategies*. Portsmouth, NH: Heinemann.

■ Hoyt, Linda, Margaret E. Mooney, and Brenda Parkes. 2003. *Exploring Informational Texts: From Theory to Practice*. Portsmouth, NH: Heinemann.

■ Owocki, Gretchen. 2012. *The Common Core Lesson Book, K–5: Working with Increasingly Complex Literature, Informational Text, and Foundational Reading Skills*. Portsmouth, NH: Heinemann.

■ Robb, Laura. 2003. *Teaching Reading in Social Studies, Science, and Math*. New York: Scholastic.

thinking about GENRE

this object → is a metaphor for → this genre		characteristics of this genre	examples of this genre
mirror, x-ray	biography & autobiography	facts about someone's life, opinions, informs about people	Life Stories of Oprah Winfrey, B. Franklin, P. Revere, L. DaVinci, J. Montana, Tiki Barber, Mystery Hunter
cereal box, photograph	image reading	fun! pictures & text, texture, visualizing while thinking (font), notice colors, shapes, details	Netflix, ESPN, McDonalds ads, wordless picture books, t-shirts, hats
prism, unicorn, elf, gnome	fantasy, tall tales, fiction (adventures)	unreal bright, unordinary, imaginative, flabbergasting	Guardians of Ga'hoole, childhood fantasy stories, Spooky old, The Ghost of Crutchfield Hall, Legends Jack Johnson, Paul Bunyon
jar, journal, baggie, line, corner, bunny	Poetry	ongoing, poetic license (Robert Frost), feelings, not limited, freestyle (young, wild & free)	Shel Silverstein, Jeff Moss, Jack Prelutsky, Edgar Allan Poe, Jennifer Cole, Judd Wendy Cope, 39 Series
clothespin, paper clip, quarter + ?	historical fiction (realistic)	fiction from history, take a story, add history, take history, add exaggeration & imagination & characters	Letters to Rifka, Titanic movie, Percy Jackson, Setting of Harry Potter, Invincible, "based on or true stories"
prop, curtain, play, puzzle piece	drama	performance, fun! emotion-packed, movement, staged, props, dialogue	Shakespeare, The Nutcracker, Stormi Giovanni, Beauty & the Beast, Romeo & Juliet
question mark?, magnifying glass, puzzle piece	mystery	an unknown, suspense, complex, twist, clues, puzzles, trick	Sherlock Holmes, Scooby Doo, Who Dun It, 39, The (thirty nine) clues

Epilogue
Only One Bean

There I was! With more Poozers than I'd ever seen! There I was!
With my shooter and only one bean! There I was!
And I thought, "Will I ever get through to the wonderful city of
Solla Sollew on the banks of the beautiful river Wah-Hoo,
where they never have troubles, at least very few?"
—from *I Had Trouble in Getting to Solla Sollew*
by Dr. Seuss (Random House, 1965)

We're surrounded by Poozers these days: anxiety-producing state tests, suffocating pacing guides, fragmented schedules, and mandatory programs. Too many of us are caught standing there with only one bean, feeling as though we can't defend ourselves, allowing others to make us believe there is only one way to teach, only one way to get to Solla Sollew.

I'm about to say something that will seem quite odd. Don't use the ideas in this book just as they are. Quickly take them, chew on them, and spit them back out as your own. Change them. Better them. Merge them with your own tried and true lessons.

This book is not a script. Don't end up with only one bean.

Works Cited

Admongo.gov. Accessed November 08, 2012. www.admongo.gov.

Alison Gopnik Homepage. Available at www.alisongopnik.com. Accessed November 08, 2012.

Barbara Lehmann Homepage. Available www.barbaralehmanbooks.com. Accessed November 08, 2012.

Barton, Bob, and David Booth. 2004. *Poetry Goes to School: From Mother Goose to Shel Silverstein*. Markham, Ont.: Pembroke Publishers.

Bayles, David, and Ted Orland. 1993. *Art & Fear: Observations on the Perils (and Rewards) of Artmaking*. Eugene, OR: The Image Continuum Press.

Bertoff, Anne. 1980. *The Making of Meaning: Metaphors, Models, and Maxims for Writing Teachers*. New Jersey: Boynton Cook.

Bomer, Katherine. 2005. *Writing a Life: Teaching Memoir to Sharpen Insight, Shape Meaning—and Triumph over Tests*. Portsmouth, NH: Heinemann.

Booth, David, and Bill Moore. 1988. *Poems Please!: Sharing Poetry with Children*. Markham, Ontario: Pembroke Publishers.

Booth, David W. 2006. *Reading Doesn't Matter Anymore: Shattering the Myths of Literacy*. Markham, Ontario: Pembroke Publishers.

Burke, Jim. 2000. *Reading Reminders: Tools, Tips, and Techniques*. Portsmouth, NH: Boynton/Cook Publishers.

Costa, Arthur L. 1991. *The School as a Home for the Mind*. Arlington, Heights, IL: Skylight Publishing.

Daniels, Harvey, and Nancy Steineke. 2011. *Texts and Lessons for Content-area Reading*. Portsmouth, NH: Heinemann.

Dr. Seuss. 1965. *I Had Trouble in Getting to Solla Sollew*. Random House.

Duke, Nell K., and V. Susan Bennett-Armistead. 2003. *Reading & Writing Informational Text in the Primary Grades*. New York: Scholastic Teaching Resources.

Ehrenworth, Mary. 2011. *A Quick Guide to Teaching Reading through Fantasy Novels, 5–8*. Portsmouth, NH: firsthand/Heinemann.

Eisner, Elliot W. 2005. "Three Rs Are Essential, But Don't Forget the A—the Arts." *The Los Angeles Times*. January.

Fletcher, Ralph J. 2011. *Mentor Author, Mentor Texts: Short Texts, Craft Notes, and Practical Classroom Uses*. Portsmouth, NH: Heinemann.

Flynn, Nick, and Shirley McPhillips. 2000. *A Note Slipped under the Door: Teaching from Poems We Love*. York, ME: Stenhouse Publishers.

Fountas, Irene C., and Gay Su Pinnell. 2012. *Genre Prompting Guide for Fiction*. Portsmouth, NH: Heinemann.

Freeman, Judy. 2007. *Once upon a Time: Using Storytelling, Creative Drama, and Reader's Theater with Children in Grades PreK–6*. Westport, CT: Libraries Unlimited.

Frey, Nancy, and Douglas Fisher. 2008. *Teaching Visual Literacy: Using Comic Books, Graphic Novels, Anime, Cartoons, and More to Develop Comprehension and Thinking Skills*. Thousand Oaks, CA: Corwin Press.

Fuhler, Carol J., and Maria P. Walther. 2007. *Literature Is Back: Using the Best Books for Teaching Readers and Writers across Genres*. New York: Scholastic.

Garner, Joan. 2006. *Wings of Fancy: Using Readers Theatre to Study Fantasy Genre*. Westport, CT: Teacher Ideas Press.

Gear, Adrienne. 2008. *Nonfiction Reading Power: Teaching Students How to Think While They Read All Kinds of Information*. Markham, Ontario: Pembroke Publishers.

Goldstein, Thalia, and Ellen Winner. 2012. "Enhancing Empathy and Theory of Mind." *Journal of Cognition and Development* 13(1): 19–37.

Gopnik, Alison. 2005. "The Real Reason Children Love Fantasy: Kids Aren't Escapists, They're Little Scientists." *SLATE*, December 20. Available at www.slate.com/articles/arts/culturebox/2005/12/the_real_reason_children_love_fantasy.html.

———. 2011. "What Do Babies Think?" TED talk filmed in July, posted in October. Available at www.ted.com/talks/alison_gopnik_what_do_babies_think.html.

Harvey, Stephanie, and Anne Goudvis. 2005. *The Comprehension Toolkit: Language and Lessons for Active Literacy*. Portsmouth, NH: firsthand/Heinemann.

Harvey, Stephanie, and Anne Goudvis. 2008. *The Primary Comprehension Toolkit: Language and Lessons for Active Literacy*. Portsmouth, NH: firsthand/Heinemann.

Harvey, Stephanie, and Harvey Daniels. 2009. *Comprehension & Collaboration: Inquiry Circles in Action*. Portsmouth, NH: Heinemann.

Heard, Georgia, and Lester L. Laminack. 2008. *Climb inside a Poem*. Portsmouth, NH: Heinemann.

Heath, Chip, and Dan Heath. 2007. *Made to Stick: Why Some Ideas Survive and Others Die*. New York: Random House.

Holbrook, Sara, and Michael Salinger. 2006. *Outspoken!: How to Improve Writing and Speaking Skills through Poetry Performance*. Portsmouth, NH: Heinemann.

Holbrook, Sara. 2005. *Practical Poetry: A Nonstandard Approach to Meeting Content-area Standards*. Portsmouth, NH: Heinemann.

Hoyt, Linda. 2002. *Make It Real: Strategies for Success with Informational Texts*. Portsmouth, NH: Heinemann.

Hoyt, Linda, Margaret E. Mooney, and Brenda Parkes. 2003. *Exploring Informational Texts: From Theory to Practice*. Portsmouth, NH: Heinemann.

Hoyt, Linda. 2003. *Navigating Informational Texts: Easy and Explicit Strategies*. Portsmouth, NH: Heinemann.

Ian Jukes Homepage. Accessed November 08, 2012. www.committedsardine.net/.

Janeczko, Paul B. 2011. *Reading Poetry in the Middle Grades: 20 Poems and Activities That Meet the Common Core Standards and Cultivate a Passion for Poetry*. Portsmouth, NH: Heinemann.

Johnston, Peter H. 2004. *Choice Words: How Our Language Affects Children's Learning*. Portland, ME: Stenhouse Publishers.

Kajder, Sara B. 2006. *Bringing the Outside In: Visual Ways to Engage Reluctant Readers*. Portland, ME: Stenhouse Publishers.

Keene, Ellin Oliver, and Harvey Daniels. 2011. *Comprehension Going Forward: Where We Are, What's Next*. Portsmouth, NH: Heinemann.

Kelner, Lenore Blank, and Rosalind M. Flynn. 2006. *A Dramatic Approach to Reading Comprehension: Strategies and Activities for Classroom Teachers*. Portsmouth, NH: Heinemann.

Kist, William. 2010. *The Socially Networked Classroom: Teaching in the New Media Age*. Thousand Oaks, CA: Corwin.

Lattimer, Heather. 2003. *Thinking through Genre: Units of Study in Reading and Writing Workshops 4–12*. Portland, ME: Stenhouse Publishers.

Lewis, J. Patrick, and Laura Robb. 2007. *Poems for Teaching in the Content Areas: 75 Powerful Poems to Enhance Your History, Geography, Science, and Math Lessons*. New York: Scholastic.

Mantione, Roberta. 2006. Foreword in *A Dramatic Approach to Reading Comprehension: Strategies and Activities for Classroom Teachers*, by Lenore Blank Kelner and Rosalind M. Flynn. Portsmouth, NH: Heinemann.

McGregor, Tanny. 2007. *Comprehension Connections: Bridges to Strategic Reading*. Portsmouth, NH: Heinemann.

Miller, Carole S., and Juliana Saxton. 2004. *Into the Story: Language in Action through Drama*. Portsmouth, NH: Heinemann.

New York Times. 2011. "Met Backtracks on Drop in Average Audience Age" By Daniel J. Wakin. ArtsBeat, The Culture at Large. February 17.

Owocki, Gretchen. 2012. *The Common Core Lesson Book, K-5: Working with Increasingly Complex Literature, Informational Text, and Foundational Reading Skills*. Portsmouth, NH: Heinemann.

Perkins, David. 1995. *Smart Schools: Better Thinking and Learning for Every Child*. New York: Free Press.

Pinnell, Gay Su, and Irene C. Fountas. 2004. *Sing a Song of Poetry: A Teaching Resource for Phonemic Awareness, Phonics, and Fluency*. Portsmouth, NH: firsthand/ Heinemann.

Podzlony, A. 2000. "Strengthening Verbal Skills Through the Use of Classroom Drama: A Clear Link. *Journal of Aesthetic Education* 34: 239–275.

Robb, Laura. 2003. *Teaching Reading in Social Studies, Science, and Math*. New York: Scholastic.

Saricks, Joyce. 2009. *Reader's Advisory Guide to Genre Fiction*. Chicago, IL: American Library Association Editions.

Serafini, Frank, and Suzette Youngs. 2008. *More (advanced) Lessons in Comprehension: Expanding Students' Understanding of All Type of Texts*. Portsmouth, NH: Heinemann.

Sipe, Lawrence R. 2008. "Learning from Illustrations in Picturebooks" in *Teaching Visual Literacy* by Nancy Frey and Douglas Fisher, editors. Thousand Oaks, CA: Corwin Press.

Swartz, Larry. 2002. *The New Dramathemes*. Markham, Ontario: Pembroke Publishers.

Tannenbaum, Judith. 2000. *Teeth, Wiggly as Earthquakes: Writing Poetry in the Primary Grades*. York, ME: Stenhouse Publishers.

Thompson, Terry. 2008. *Adventures in Graphica: Using Comics and Graphic Novels to Teach Comprehension, 2–6*. Portland, ME: Stenhouse Publishers.

Thurman, Mark, and Emily Hearn. 2010. *Get Graphic!: Using Storyboards to Write and Draw Picture Books, Graphic Novels, or Comic Strips*. Markham, Ontario: Pembroke Publishers.

Tishman, Shari. 2008. "The Object of Their Attention." *Educational Leadership* 65(5): 44–46.

Trelease, Jim. 1982. *The Read-aloud Handbook*. Harmondsworth, Middlesex, England: Penguin Books.

Verducci, S. 2000. "A Moral Method? Thoughts on Cultivating Empathy Through Method Acting." *Journal of Moral Education* 29 (1): 87–99.

Walling, Donovan R. 2005. *Visual Knowing: Connecting Art and Ideas across the Curriculum*. Thousand Oaks, CA: Corwin Press.

Wilhelm, Jeffrey D. 2004. *Reading Is Seeing: Learning to Visualize Scenes, Characters, Ideas, and Text Worlds to Improve Comprehension and Reflective Reading*. New York: Scholastic.

Wormeli, Rick. 2009. *Metaphors & Analogies: Power Tools for Teaching Any Subject*. Portland, ME: Stenhouse Publishers.

Zarian, Beth Bartleson. 2004. *Around the World with Historical Fiction and Folktales: Highly Recommended and Award-winning Books, Grades K–8*. Lanham, MD: Scarecrow Press.

Zarnowski, Myra. 2003. *History Makers: A Questioning Approach to Reading and Writing Biographies*. Portsmouth, NH: Heinemann.

Index